THE TEN COMMANDMENTS

Exodus 20:2-14, inclusive

I am the Lord thy God, who brought thee out of the land of Egypt, out of the house of bondage.

Thou shalt have no other gods before Me. Thou shalt not make unto thee a graven image, nor any manner of likeness, of any thing that is in heaven above, or that is in the earth beneath, or that is in the water under the earth; thou shalt not bow down unto them, nor serve them; for I the Lord thy God am a jealous God, visiting the iniquity of the fathers upon the children unto the third and fourth generation of them that hate Me; and showing mercy unto the thousandth generation of them that love Me and keep My commandments.

Thou shalt not take the name of the Lord thy God in vain; for the Lord will not hold him guiltless that taketh His name in vain.

Remember the sabbath day, to keep it holy. Six days shalt thou labour, and do all thy work; but the seventh day is a sabbath unto the Lord thy God, in it thou shalt not do any manner of work, thou, nor thy son, nor thy daughter, nor thy man-servant, nor thy maid-servant, nor thy cattle, nor thy stranger that is within thy gates; for in six days the Lord made heaven and earth, the sea, and all that in them is, and rested on the seventh day; wherefore the Lord blessed the sabbath day, and hallowed it.

Honour thy father and thy mother, that thy days may be long upon the land which the Lord thy God giveth thee.

Thou shalt not murder.

Thou shalt not commit adultery.

Thou shalt not steal.

Thou shalt not bear false witness against thy neighbour.

Thou shalt not covet thy neighbour's house; thou shalt not covet thy neighbour's wife, nor his man-servant, nor his maid-servant, nor his ox, nor his ass, nor any thing that is thy neighbour's.

Courtesy of Eleanor and Jack Resler

THE JEWISH HERITAGE SERIES

THE STORY OF
THE JEWISH WAY OF LIFE

MEYER LEVIN *novelist and playwright*

TOBY K. KURZBAND *principal, New York City Public Schools*
Educational Director, Jewish Community Center, White Plains, N. Y.

STEPHEN KRAFT *art editor*

HARRY LAZARUS *illustrations*

BEHRMAN HOUSE, INC. PUBLISHERS   NEW YORK, N.Y.

Acknowledgments

The authors would like to express their appreciation to the many individuals who have been helpful in the preparation of this volume:

To Dr. Emanuel Gamoran and to the late Dr. Jacob S. Golub as the sponsors of the Demonstration School conducted jointly by the Union of American Hebrew Congregations and the Jewish Education Committee of New York in classes held at the West End Synagogue in New York and developed later in the participating schools of the Curriculum Workshop.

To Rabbi Lawrence W. Schwartz of the Jewish Community Center of White Plains, N. Y. and the members of the Religious School Committee who encouraged the development of the course during the many years while one of the authors was Educational Director of this congregation. To Rabbi Kenneth E. Stein, who made many valuable suggestions for the improvement of this course while he was Associate Rabbi of this congregation.

To the teachers of the course at the Demonstration School, the Curriculum Workshop, and the Religious School of the Jewish Community Center of White Plains, and especially to those teachers who developed phases of the course into units that appeared in the "Jewish Teacher."

To Dr. Azriel Eisenberg, and to Rabbi Paul Steinberg, for their penetrating criticism of an early manuscript and for their many pertinent questions and suggestions.

To Ruth Salinger Hyman and Rabbi Emanuel Green whose erudition and perceptive judgement added immeasurably to the completion of the book.

To Ellen Rudin, whose unique skill and sensitivity in editing made her contribution a truly creative one.

To Rabbi Morrison D. Bial, whose scholarship proved invaluable when he undertook to evaluate and edit the manuscript through all its stages.

To Robin King and Frances Long, for their own special contribution to the book.

And to Jacob Behrman, our publisher.

TOBY K. KURZBAND
MEYER LEVIN

New York, 1959

Foreword to the Teacher

THE AUTHORS OF THIS VOLUME are extremely gratified by the response of Jewish schools to "The Story of the Synagogue," their first volume in The Jewish Heritage Series. Its adoption as a textbook by many schools, and the words of appreciation from principals, teachers, pupils, and parents, are accepted as an indication of the validity of its approach to the curriculum of the Intermediate grades.

This approach stems from the belief that children learn best when their educational experiences begin with their immediate environment and employ materials that are both meaningful and enjoyable to them. From experiences of this type, the children can then be led into an appreciation of the events and personalities that make up our Jewish heritage.

In this second volume, we have again begun with the immediate experience of the child by making him aware that he has a "way of life" which he shares with his family, his schoolmates and with all the other individuals and groups with whom he comes into contact. Within this way of life, he also has a "Jewish way of life," which is the sum of all the experiences that grow out of his attendance in a Jewish school, his family's membership in a congregation, the observance of Judaism in his home and the ethical values that guide him in his daily life.

Awareness of the differences among the Jews in his own community helps the child understand that Jewish ways of life have undergone many changes throughout the long history of the Jewish people and still differ considerably in the many lands where Jews live today.

However, as the common origin of the Jewish way of life is traced back to the Bible and the Talmud, the commentaries, the responsa and the codes, it becomes apparent that the basic unity of the Jewish way of life is greater than any of the differences that may exist at the moment.

Since these differences reflect the efforts of each Jewish community to live as Jews in varying environments, the greatest attention is given to the Eastern European Jewish community in the 17th to the 19th centuries, to Western Europe and America in the 19th and 20th centuries, and to the development of an old-new way of Jewish life in contemporary Israel.

The book ends with the relationship of Judaism to other religions and to the common problems which all religions must face. And because it is addressed to the child reader, it ends also by pointing out to him that each generation develops its own Jewish way of life and that he too may look ahead to writing the next chapter in this story.

The questions at the end of each chapter should serve to stimulate pupils' thinking on the many problems and issues that are relevant to their own lives. Those questions which the pupils are to address to their parents are intended to help the parent serve as a resource in the educational process as well as involving parents in facing with their children the implications of living a full Jewish life in the home.

With the help of a supplementary Activity Book by Abraham Segal, it is hoped that the teacher will find this course a rich and lively experience for himself as well as for his pupils.

TOBY K. KURZBAND

Contents

Maps and Time Lines

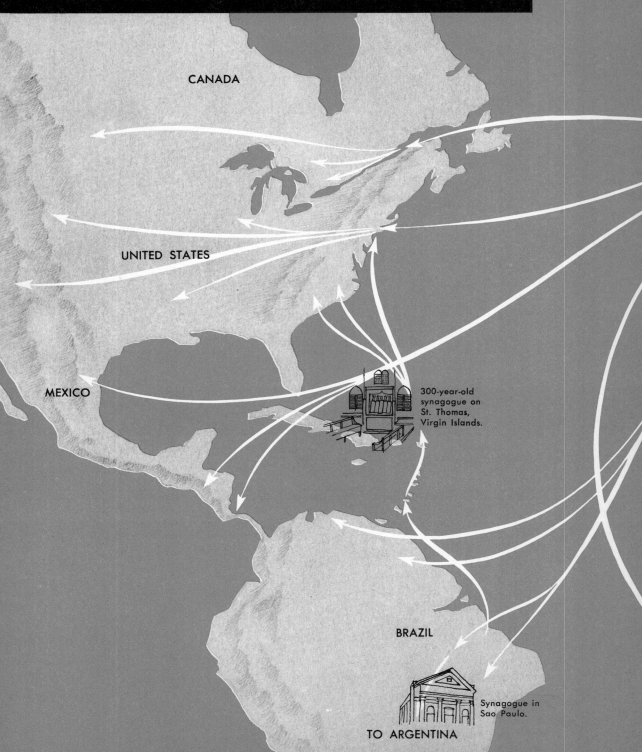

CANADA

UNITED STATES

MEXICO

300-year-old
synagogue on
St. Thomas,
Virgin Islands.

BRAZIL

Synagogue in
Sao Paulo.

TO ARGENTINA

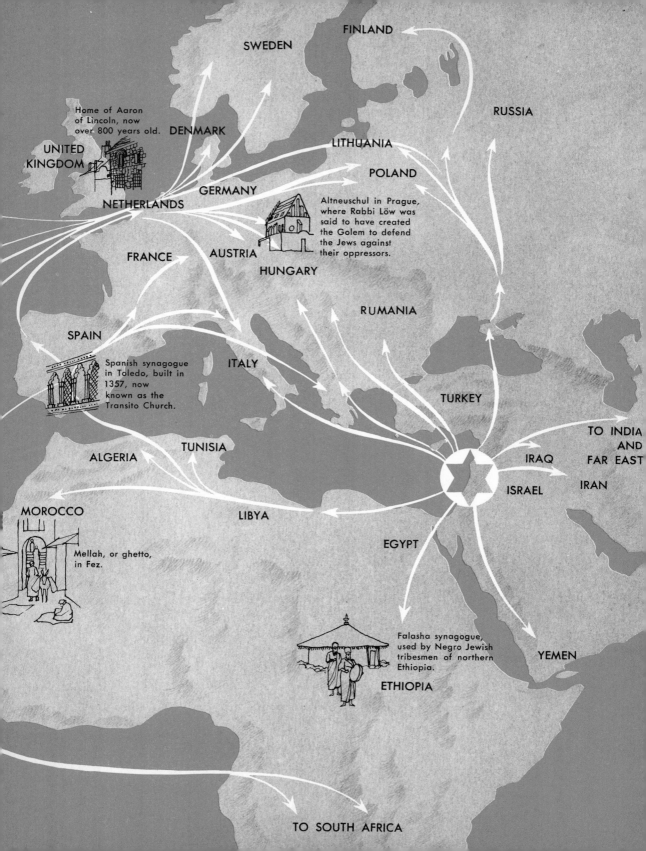

SWEDEN

FINLAND

UNITED KINGDOM

Home of Aaron of Lincoln, now over 800 years old.

DENMARK

RUSSIA

LITHUANIA

POLAND

NETHERLANDS

GERMANY

Altneuschul in Prague, where Rabbi Löw was said to have created the Golem to defend the Jews against their oppressors.

FRANCE

AUSTRIA

HUNGARY

RUMANIA

SPAIN

Spanish synagogue in Toledo, built in 1357, now known as the Transito Church.

ITALY

TURKEY

TO INDIA AND FAR EAST

IRAQ

IRAN

ISRAEL

ALGERIA

TUNISIA

MOROCCO

Mellah, or ghetto, in Fez.

LIBYA

EGYPT

YEMEN

Falasha synagogue, used by Negro Jewish tribesmen of northern Ethiopia.

ETHIOPIA

TO SOUTH AFRICA

For Rinna / *For Jacob and Anna Kurzband*

What we mean by "the Jewish Ways of Life"

CHAPTER I

What is a Way of Life?

Did you ever wonder what makes you what you are? Suppose you had been born an Indian, or an Eskimo, or a Frenchman. Your whole way of life would be different. If someone asks you, "What makes you different from an Eskimo?" you'd have to answer, "It isn't just the clothes I wear, or the language I speak, or living in an igloo. It's everything I do."

It would be the songs you sing, the things you eat and the way you cook them, your beliefs and customs and rules—everything taken together makes up a way of life.

How does a way of life get started? In many ways it is like starting a club. If you got together to form a club, you would start with your schoolmates, or your neighborhood friends, children who already have something in common with you. Then you would say, "Let's have some rules." You might say, "Let's have a password." Or, "Let's all dress alike," or "Let's wear the same pin."

Pretty soon your club group would have a little way of life of its own.

Aside from a club, there are groups to which you belong without ever thinking about your "membership." There is one group to which every person belongs from the moment he is born. That is the family.

You might say that the person is initiated by being born. And soon even a baby discovers that a family has rules and regulations. There are rules about when to eat and when to sleep, when to go outdoors and what to wear, even for a baby. And these rules are different in different places in the world, for each place has its own way of life.

We belong to many groups

As a child grows, he may join many kinds of groups. He may go to the same playground every day and meet and play with the same children. That is a group, even if it is not organized into a regular club, because the same children will usually be there at the same hours, and play in a certain way. They will take turns with the ball, or they may choose up sides, and they will say, "This is how we do it."

When you first started school, you belonged to a new group. You belonged to a class. And you also belonged to the school. And outside of the school, you may now belong to the Scouts, to a club of friends and of course, to your religious school class.

As you grow up and go to high school and college you may belong to other kinds of clubs—sports clubs, dramatic clubs, social clubs. And an adult can have still more groups to belong to.

Have you heard your mother say she has to go to a sisterhood meeting, or a bridge club meeting, or a parent-teachers meeting?

Have you heard your father say he has to go to a meeting of his lodge, or his professional society, or his union, or his bowling club? Or of the war veterans, or of his political party?

You see, the life of a person can be pictured by the groups to which he belongs. And in each group, he is expected to behave according to rules

Your family belongs to many groups

and customs. If you put together all the customs of all the groups to which a person belongs in his life, that is his way of life.

Customs are the habits of a people

Every group has its "right way" of doing things. Most of these ways become automatic, like our habit of standing when we hear the "Star Spangled Banner." You don't even stop to think about these everyday ways, any more than you think about how to use your knife and fork. And yet even the way you use your knife and fork would be different if you lived in Europe, where the fork is always kept in the left hand. And in China you would use chopsticks.

Most things about our way of life are so much a habit that we don't even think about them. In your family there are many regulations that are so natural you forget you ever had to learn them. There may be a certain place at the table for each member of the family. You may have a certain custom about who does the serving, and in what turn people are served. You may have a tradition of eating certain foods at certain times, like chicken every Friday night.

Sometimes such things are thought of as customs, and sometimes they are actually put down as rules. In baseball, for instance, there is a complicated set of rules, set down in an official rulebook. But each team may also have its own customs, as long as they are not against the official rules. A team might have a certain song it sings before each game. Why? "Because we always do it."

Written and unwritten laws

There are two kinds of laws, the written and unwritten. An "unwritten law" means an old custom of doing things, that people have always felt is right. A play group on the playground, for instance, may not have any laws or rules written down. Still, everybody *knows* it is right to take turns and to give the other players a chance.

But a Scout group does have a written law; it has a "Code." And in the same way, from your city to your state, all the way up to the United States, there are written codes and laws. Even the United Nations has its laws: the United Nations Charter.

At the very top of all our laws are our religious laws. In religion, also, there are many customs which people explain only by saying, "That's the way its always been done." But the customs and ceremonies in a religion are there to help us remember the actual laws of the religion.

These laws are older than all the government laws on earth, for they are the original laws about what is right and what is wrong. For instance, "Thou Shalt Not Kill" is a religious law, and it later became a law made by every civilized government. For government laws about the most important things in life are usually meant to carry out the same ideas as the religious laws about right and wrong.

Thus all groups have rules, written or unwritten, and both kinds of rules tell you how to live. Often what an individual learns in one group will be a part of what he does in another group.

A person who learns to be courteous at home, and in school, will usually be courteous when he is with his friends, and also with strangers. A person who learns to do "good deeds" as a Scout will do good deeds whenever he can. A person who learns to obey the Ten Commandments will obey the laws of society as he grows up. And all the rules and customs about how to live, taken together, make up your way of life.

The American way of life

As you have already seen, a person belongs to many groups at the same time, in school, at home, in the synagogue. As members of the synagogue, we belong to the Jewish group. But all of us in this country are also a part of the American group.

Americans are a combination of people from all over the world, and the American way of life is a combination of all their ways of life. When an election is going on, we hear many speeches about this "American way of life." We are reminded that we believe that everybody should have an even chance to get the good things of life, and that there should be more and more good things for more and more people.

Our American life has its holidays, like the Fourth of July. As Americans, we celebrate the Fourth because that is the day on which the people who live in this land declared their freedom to   *15* have their own government.

Besides our national holidays, which all of us share, almost every American has religious holidays which he celebrates. But not all of us celebrate the same ones, for not all of us have the same religion.

One thing which we enjoy as Americans is our freedom of religion. That means that everyone is free to belong to the religion of his choice.

So as you know, there are Christians who have a Christian way of life joined with their American way of life. The Christian part is celebrated in holidays like Christmas and Easter. It is observed in their churches and Sunday schools. In Christian homes, there are books and music and prayers that form a part of their religion.

And we Jews join our Jewish way of life to the American way of life. Our Jewish way of life flows from generations and generations. We can follow

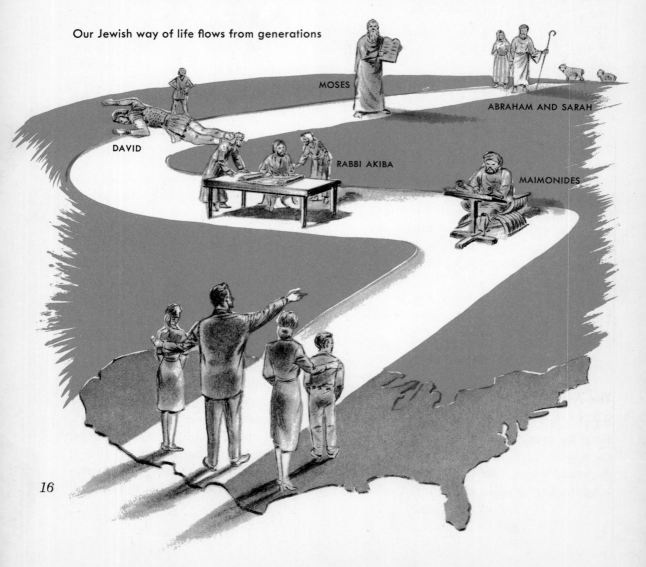

Our Jewish way of life flows from generations

MOSES

ABRAHAM AND SARAH

DAVID

RABBI AKIBA

MAIMONIDES

16

the course straight back to Abraham. And this is the stream we belong to; it gives us our Jewish identity.

An identity inside of an identity

Every American has another identity, inside of his identity as an American. The identity of a person goes back as far as can be found out, through all the ancestors who have made him what he is. So Americans will say, "My folks came from England, way back," or, "I'm Irish," or, "I'm Catholic."

And when you say, "I'm Jewish," that is your identity inside of your identity as an American. It means your ancestors go way back to the time of the Bible, before there were Americans, and even before there was an English language.

And many of the beliefs your ancestors had are part of our own way of life as Jews and Americans today.

For each people keeps many customs from the past in its present way of life. These customs often come down to us in our religion and in our family habits, and as they come down, they also change.

In this book we will learn what are the ways of the Jews, and how these ways have been kept alive in the teachings of the Jewish religion. You will see that many things you feel you always knew, came to you as part of your Jewish way of life. You will learn how all the things you do and hope are part of your Jewish way of life.

Why we tell of Jewish "ways" of life

But you may be wondering, "If there is a Jewish way of life, why don't all Jews do things in exactly the same way?"

You will see that Jews in other lands, and even Jews in your own community, have a number of customs that are different from your own. But you will see what is more important—that all these customs are based on the same deep beliefs that fit together and form the Jewish religion.

That is why we speak not only of the Jewish way of life but of the Jewish "ways" of life.

What are the things that are the same, and what are the things that are somewhat different, in the Jewish ways of life?

THINKING ABOUT WHAT YOU HAVE LEARNED

1. Each person's "way of life" is made up of all the groups to which he belongs. Which groups have been most important in your "way of life"?
2. The oldest rules of life are religious laws. How many Jewish religious laws can you name that have become laws of our government?

QUESTIONS TO ASK YOUR PARENTS

1. Why is freedom of religion so important a part of the American way of life? Do Jews in all lands have this freedom?
2. Every family has its own rules. Would it be a good idea if your family had its rules posted so that everyone could see them?

CHAPTER II

Jewish Ways of Life

Your Jewish school

You are reading this book because you go to a Jewish school, and the Jewish school is a part of your Jewish way of life. All the things you do in this school and in your synagogue are part of it.

You celebrate Jewish holidays, you attend Jewish worship service, you give money to help other Jews. You read the Bible and other Jewish books, you may study Hebrew and you discuss what Jews believe.

What you do at home

And at home you do many things that are part of your Jewish way of life. You celebrate the holidays with your family. There are Jewish books in your house as well as other books, and Jewish records as well as other records.

There are candlesticks for the Sabbath. And the Hanukah menorah. Perhaps you have pictures of Israel, or things that were made in Israel. And perhaps you have an old family Bible in Hebrew, and a prayer book.

And then, you know about Jewish cooking and special good things to eat, like latkes for Hanukah. You know about hamentashen, the poppyseed cakes of Purim, and you know about honey candies, called taiglach, for Rosh Hashanah. And you know how people from other ways of life love to taste real Jewish dishes such as gefilte fish.

Not only things you eat, but even some things you talk about often come from your Jewish way of life. You will notice that at home, and with your friends, you talk with special interest about things concerning Jews.

Sometimes there is news about Israel in the paper, or about famous American Jews, like news about a scientist winning the Nobel Prize. Perhaps a Jew is elected a governor. Your family will pick out these stories and talk about them. Or there may be notice of a meeting to help Jews who are in need. Your parents will discuss what should be done to help them.

Then, there are the big family events in the Jewish way of life. Times when

Rehearsing for a Purim play

the whole family attends worship service together, or attends a Bar Mitzvah, or a wedding. Sometimes these ceremonies take place partly in the synagogue and partly at home, or at a big meeting hall; and there will be good food and music. And sometimes the event may be a Jewish funeral, when everyone goes to the Jewish cemetery. All this is part of the way of life of our people.

Differences outside, agreements inside

And yet you know that not all Jews go to the same kind of synagogue, and you know that some Jews do things differently from the customary way of doing them in your own family. You may begin by thinking, "Those Jews do things the wrong way. I wonder if they know it?"

Or you might sometimes get the idea that you yourself are doing things the wrong way. For example, you might feel that you are wrong if you walk into an Orthodox Jewish home and find that all the men and boys are wearing hats.

But a way of life is not so simple. A way of life is a very large idea. And it can hold many varieties of life inside itself, and it can even hold some contradictions.

There are the outside things about a way of life, such as the clothes we wear, and there are the inside things, such as the ideas we believe in. While the Jewish ways of life may differ about some outside things, our inside beliefs are the same.

19

Poland and Yemen

But like the people who practice it, a way of life keeps changing and growing.

Two hundred years ago in Poland, if you had gone into a little Jewish town, you would have found that there were few differences among the Jews of that town. They dressed alike; the men all had beards. And everybody had exactly the same rules about kosher food, and about the time for prayers and the words to say in each prayer.

So even the idea of having differences, as we have in America today, is an example of how a way of life grows and changes. We Jews in America have differences right in the same place, in the same country and the same city.

But in the old days there were only differences among Jews in different places. If you had gone travelling two hundred years ago, you would have found that while the Jews of Poland were alike, they were quite different from the Jews of Italy or far-away Yemen.

For the Jews of Yemen would all have been behaving in an ancient way. Their way was said to be much the same as it was in the days of King Solomon. Yet they had the same deep beliefs as the Jews of other lands and all their ways were Jewish ways of life.

No matter how they are dressed or what language they talk, Jews believe the same main ideas. They may wear

The Jewish way of life varies

POLAND

YEMEN

shorts like Israelis, or suits like Americans, but they have the same ideas about God and justice.

Jewish ways of life differ today

If a teacher in everyday school says, "Give your definition of liberty," no two children would use exactly the same words. But all of them would have a general understanding of liberty. And so it is with Judaism.

The child who sits next to you in religious school may not have exactly the same Jewish way of life as you, even though both of you belong to the same synagogue. He may come to services more often than you do. He may celebrate Jewish holidays a little differently at home.

ISRAEL

That is because there are now different customs about all this, all inside the same Jewish community. For example —hats. This is about the first thing we all notice. At some synagogues, men wear hats; at others, they take off their hats.

And as you know, in some synagogues women sit apart from the men, usually in a balcony. But in other synagogues, even if the men wear hats, the men and women sit together. So it seems that these rules and customs are mixed up.

And if you listen to the service, you will find that in one synagogue it is entirely in Hebrew, and in another it is partly in English and partly in Hebrew.

You might think that the Jewish way of life is not very clear. Or, you might say that these are all Jewish ways, as long as people go to the synagogue and believe in the Jewish idea of God and the Jewish ideas of right and wrong.

Judaism is alive

What do the differences in Jewish ways of life show us? For one thing, they show us that Judaism is very much alive.

In the thousands of years of Judaism, the Jews moved from one country to another. The people in one place changed the rules a bit, and the people in another country interpreted the rules differently. But these changes never altered the main idea behind the holidays and the services. That main idea is Judaism.

Later on, we will learn how Judaism is observed in the United States by three types of synagogues. They are called Orthodox, Conservative and Reform, because they have differences in their services and ceremonies.

Respecting our differences

And there are differences in Jewish homes, particularly in the way Jewish food is prepared. In some homes, the food is not different from the food in the homes of non-Jewish neighbors. In others, the rules about what is kosher are strictly kept. A Reform Jew may visit the home of an Orthodox friend, where no milk is served when meat is served. Of course, he will not ask for milk, because we all respect each other's ways.

Some Jews do not often take part in worship. They may belong to Jewish community groups that are helping other Jews in need; they may be especially interested in Jewish history, or Jewish music, art or literature; they may study the Bible in their own way. Even though they do not attend services regularly, still they live according to the Jewish ideas of doing right and being charitable.

These main ideas, about which Jews of all kinds agree, make up Judaism. They are the great do's and don't's of life. A Jew feels at home in his way of life when he understands these ideas, because they help him always to decide what he should and what he should not do.

Where did these ideas come from?

Prophets and wise men

In the beginning, our inspired prophets brought us these ideas from God. In the long history of the Jewish people, great leaders and teachers have tried to explain what each man should do in life, and how Jews may carry out the laws which God commanded. And so, when a problem comes in a Jew's life, he asks, "Hasn't this problem come before? And how was it solved?"

He may find the answer in what he has learned in his Jewish school, or in the synagogue, or in books. Or in talking with a rabbi or another wise person, or in advice from his own family. He may find the answer in his own thoughts that come from all these sources put together—from his way of life.

Your Judaism helps you in every decision you make. Every time you decide what is fair and what is not fair, you are carrying on thoughts that may go all the way back to Abraham. That is what it means to be part of the Jewish way of life and to have it be part of you.

Now, what are these basic ideas that make up Judaism? What are the basic ideas that make up your Jewish way of life?

THINKING ABOUT WHAT YOU HAVE LEARNED

1. How long a list can you write of things you have learned in your Jewish school that make up your Jewish way of life?
2. If you have a friend who belongs to a different synagogue, see if you can discover which of the things he does as you do and which he does differently.

QUESTIONS TO ASK YOUR PARENTS

1. Ask your parents to tell you how their Jewish way of life today differs from their Jewish way of life when they were your age. Are different "Jewish ways of life" in your community a good thing?

CHAPTER III

The Beliefs inside the Jewish Way of Life

Choosing between right and wrong

We have seen that a way of life can be made up of customs and rules and ceremonies. But these are only outer things that express the beliefs inside of us, and our way of thinking.

Jews believe that whenever a Jewish person has to think and decide what is right and what is wrong, his knowledge of Judaism will help him make the right choice.

What is this knowledge of Judaism? And how do we get it?

It is actually a knowledge that grows out of the long history of the Jewish people. Every great leader, beginning with Abraham, has sought to find out how to know what is right, and what is wrong. Moses was called the Law-Giver because he set down our first great rules about right and wrong. Every rabbi seeks to teach this knowledge all his life. And every wise Jew may add a thought or an idea to our whole understanding of what is right and what is wrong.

All this, put together, is Judaism. This does not mean that to live as a good Jew you will have to read and study what every single rabbi said and what every wise man thought. But for most of us, this means that all these thoughts, all this wisdom is carried along by the whole Jewish people. And if you are living in the Jewish way of life you will be carried along by the experience of your people, too.

All this wisdom of the Jews keeps growing from the main ideas of Judaism.

The belief in one God

The first and basic idea of Judaism is about God. It is a truth that was first understood and told to others by Abraham, and that was the beginning of Judaism.

Abraham saw that there was one God who was the creator of the world and of man.

Abraham saw that all creation was one, and that man was the pinnacle of

Man..."little lower than the angels"

all the living beings of flesh and blood created in this world. Man had a spirit; he could think and feel and strive to tell right from wrong. And because man shared in the life of the spirit, Abraham understood that man was made in the image of God.

This was the beginning of Judaism.

There are other religions that tell of the one God. Indeed, today the great religions of the world tell of the one God. Each religion has its own way of coming to this understanding, and Judaism is our way because our people have kept together in a direct link, from family to family, all the way back to Abraham. And each of us can almost feel the joy and the wonder that Abraham felt when he saw the truth.

The holy quality of man

From Abraham onward, our prophets were inspired, and they pictured the spiritual world for us. They pictured the ideas of goodness and truth and love and purity, and these spiritual ideas they called the holy part of man. They said that man was created in the image of God, that he should be merciful, just and loving.

The prophets saw that man, in his soul, possessed these holy qualities but he did not possess them perfectly. Man was also a bodily creature of the earth, and because of his bodily needs and his earthly desires he sometimes did things that were ugly and hurtful. So they saw that in the order of creation, man stood lower than the angels. Yet 25

The family is the center of Jewish life

he was made in the image of God; he contained a spark of creation. And he could strive to become more perfect in his ways.

Life and family are sacred

Because man contained a spark of creation, because he was made in God's image, man's life was sacred. That is how the Jews came to believe in the sanctity of human life.

And that is why Abraham understood that the people all around him, the people of those times, were acting like savages when they sacrificed human lives on altars to their many gods.

And because man's life was sacred, since man alone of all the creatures on earth could come so close to God, then the source of man's life was sacred.

The Jews thus came to the idea of the sanctity of the family. They saw that family love was precious because from the love of the mother and father came the child. And in love of the family, the understanding of God could be passed from generation to generation.

You may believe that everybody knows this today, and that this knowledge comes naturally to everyone. It comes naturally to you because it is part of your Jewish way of life.

It has also become part of many other ways of life; so you see this same idea among the Christians, and all around you. But there are still places on the earth where family life is not very important, where children are merely part of the larger group, and can hardly pick out their parents. For Jews, the family is the center of life, and Jewish children honor their parents for having given them life and having taught them the basic ideas of humanity.

The idea of justice

After discovering their ideas of God and of the spiritual qualities that link man to God, our ancestors came to the

26

basic idea of justice between their fellow men.

You may be surprised to find that the idea of justice was not always accepted everywhere. But among primitive people and savages, might makes right. The strongest decides what the others shall do, even though the others may not feel it to be fair.

But when the Jews understood that every human life is sacred, they came to understand that there was equality in every human life, and that the weak persons had to be protected from the stronger persons, so that they could have their right share in the world. Thus, Jews began to make rules about payment for labor. And the first rules that we know of about the freeing of slaves were made by the Jews.

It took a very long time to develop these ideas of justice, and even today they are far from perfect. But long ago it became part of the Jewish way of life that every man could ask for justice. The poorest man could go up against the king himself, and ask for justice. We can see this in the Bible story of Naboth's vineyard, when the prophet Elijah stood before King Ahab and told him that a king could do wrong if he took away what belonged to another man.

You can see how unusual this is when you think of the many tales you read about kings and princes in the history of the world. No one dared say a king could do wrong, for fear of having his head cut off. Yet among Jews, a king could be told he was wrong, because the idea of justice was as important as life itself.

Jews have never lost sight of this idea. All of our scholars, and all of our wise men, and rabbis, and every Jew in himself, devote themselves to making more perfect our understanding of what is fair, what is just, what is right, what is wrong.

Peace between men and nations

When we understand that justice itself is sacred, because man is sacred, then we come to the next basic idea of Judaism, the idea of peace between nations.

Among savage people the way to settle a quarrel between one man and another was by fighting, even killing.

Elijah confronts King Ahab

But when the idea of justice arose among the Jews and they understood that people could live according to laws, then they believed that nations, too, could some day settle their quarrels without fighting.

But you may wonder, "Didn't the Jews have wars, and aren't we told that they are good fighters, too?" Yes, when Jews have had to fight, they have proved good warriors. But even in old times they did not often start wars as many other nations did, merely for the sake of conquering other people.

In the history of the world, again and again there have been nations whose leaders tried to conquer other people, and even the whole world. In the ancient times of the Jews, Abraham sought a land where he could be free to worship God, and so he came into the Promised Land, with his flocks. He was a man of peace, as we know by the story of the well of Beersheba,

MEDITERRANEAN SEA

28   EGYPT

The land of Israel stood between the giants of east and west where Abraham watered his flocks. Another tribe came there for water and rather than quarrel, Abraham dug a different well.

The Jews lived in the Promised Land, but during a famine they went to Egypt. And when, long afterward, Moses led the Jews back to their land, they had to fight to regain it. But they never went out to conquer other lands than their own.

Their own land was small, and it lay between the great nations of the east and the west, between Syria and Egypt. The east and the west took turns in trying to conquer each other, and they would march over the land to get at each other. Perhaps that was why the Jews came to believe so deeply that nations should not try to conquer other nations, but should live in peace with each other.

Finally the Jews were driven from their own country, and they were scattered over the world. And through the centuries, although they had to fight as soldiers, they understood that there should be no wars. That nations, like men, should understand the sanctity of human life and try to settle their problems by peaceful means. And so the Jewish prophets, even in ancient times, prophesied that the time of peace would come: "Nation shall not lift up sword against nation, neither shall they learn war any more." Jews believe in this, and strive to make that time come.

ASSYRIA

BABYLONIA

The ideas of forgiveness and mercy

If men are to mend their quarrels, and to accept justice, they must be able to forgive each other. They must feel mercy toward those who have been wrong or who have acted badly, just as God is merciful toward the evil done by men.

And this is one of the basic beliefs of Judaism. It is so important that we have a special day each year when we can forgive all our enemies and ask for forgiveness for our own wrongs. That day as you know is Yom Kippur. It is a time when each man says to anyone with whom he had quarreled, "Let us

29

forgive each other, and let us start all over."

The idea of tzedakah

If we know how to be merciful and to forgive, and we know that others are merciful to us, and forgive us, then we understand another of the basic ideas of Judaism, the idea of charity. In Judaism, charity is more than a gift from

just out of extra goodness or kindness, but a necessary part of his life.

The search for knowledge

In the same way, it is a necessary part of a Jew's life to keep on searching for and learning what is right. In the Jewish way of life, this search is never ended. The search to know God's meaning and

the better off to the worse off. Charity has a special word, *tzedakah*, and it means doing what is right.

For the Jew who is fortunate enough to have what he needs understands that it is only right to give away part of it to the needy.

We know that in Judaism every man is considered responsible for his brothers. Helping those who are less fortunate is not something that a Jew does

God's way is a search for all knowledge, in science, in history, in art, in nature. Throughout the ages, the Jews have been noted for their love of learning.

Joy in living

That love of learning is a love of life itself. It brings joy in living because it helps us to understand and to live in harmony with God's world. Judaism is a way of enlightenment. Judaism seeks to grow away from the dark fears of the savage world. Judaism teaches us to find joy in living, to love song and beauty and the good things of the earth, to find joy with our fellow men as with our families. Our religion tells that man is made in God's image, and as he

of life, within the American way, is composed of the basic ideas in our religion and the long experience of our people. These ideas teach us that man is made in the image of God, who created him and created the world. Man is different from other creatures, because he partakes of the spirit of creation, and therefore human life is sacred, and the family that carries forward human life is sacred.

comes closer to that image he feels great joy and happiness.

What we have learned in this chapter

Thus we have seen that we are guided in everything we do by our way of life. Our way of life in America is composed of the ways of all the people who came together in this land to create freedom and abundance. And our Jewish way

Peace, brotherhood and good deeds are basic to the Jewish way of life

And the sanctity of human life must be protected through justice that brings peace between men and between nations. Justice teaches us mercy and forgiveness, and gratitude for good fortune reminds us that it is our duty to share our goods with the less fortunate.

In our way of life, we strive always to learn, to discover, to study and to enrich our spirits with knowledge. This brings us closer to understanding God's ways, so that our own way of life may have the greatest harmony with the universe. And in this we find joy, the great joy of living.

Back to the beginnings

In our next unit of study, we will see how the Jewish ways of life began and grew and changed, and why they are as we know them today. We can learn how they used to be by going back to the books that were used in olden times, the books that told Jews how they should guide their lives. In those books we will find the beginnings of our Jewish ideas and beliefs. As we read, it will be almost as though we were living in those times, and that, like the whole Jewish people, we have kept on living right into our own day.

THINKING ABOUT WHAT YOU HAVE LEARNED

1. The Bible says that man was created in the image of God. Does that mean that God looks like a man? What do you think it means?
2. Think of one act you have done this year to carry out one of the basic Jewish beliefs.

QUESTIONS TO ASK YOUR PARENTS

1. Why is the importance of the family a basic belief in Judaism?
2. The time of peace still hasn't come to the world, even though our prophets spoke of it 2500 years ago. Today the United Nations is man's hope for peace. Discuss with your parents the role of the U.N. in achieving peace.

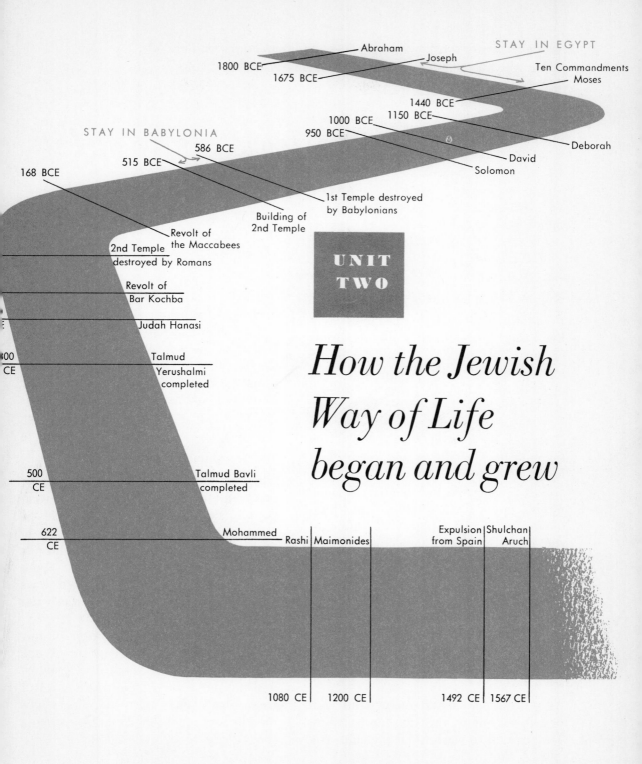

Abraham

1800 BCE

Joseph

1675 BCE

STAY IN EGYPT

Ten Commandments
Moses

1440 BCE

1150 BCE

1000 BCE

950 BCE

Deborah

David

Solomon

STAY IN BABYLONIA

586 BCE

515 BCE

168 BCE

1st Temple destroyed
by Babylonians

Building of
2nd Temple

Revolt of
the Maccabees

2nd Temple
destroyed by Romans

Revolt of
Bar Kochba

Judah Hanasi

400
CE

Talmud
Yerushalmi
completed

500
CE

Talmud Bavli
completed

622
CE

Mohammed

Rashi

Maimonides

Expulsion
from Spain

Shulchan
Aruch

1080 CE

1200 CE

1492 CE

1567 CE

UNIT TWO

How the Jewish Way of Life began and grew

CHAPTER IV

The Jewish Way of Life begins with the Torah

A book of stories, history and law

In all the lands where the Jews have lived, and through all these hundreds of years, we said they kept the same ideas about life. They kept their idea of God, and of man's nearness to God, and of justice. How do we know they kept these ideas? Because they carried a sacred book with them, which we know—a book of stories and history and law, called the Torah.

As the years passed and life became more complicated, and as the Jews moved to different places, the rules in the Torah had to be explained. These explanations were written down in books. If we read these books we can see how the Jews lived from one age to the next. And we can see that they kept their main ideas, even though their daily life changed as time went on.

Do's and don't's

As soon as you could understand, you began to follow the do's and don't's. You learned to wash to keep clean. You learned to eat certain food to keep healthy. You learned to play fair.

Your combination of do's and don't's is part of the way of life we have been talking about. Some of the do's and don't's are rules. Some of them are customs. Some of them are traditions. All of them together guide your behavior.

The Ten Commandments

The strongest rules of all are called commandments. And when the Jewish people was in its infancy, it received a set of commandments from on high. These commandments are the main pillars of the Jewish way of life. Some people believe that all civilized laws have been thought out from these ten main rules.

These ten rules are written in our Torah. In fact, they are written twice in the Torah, in the part called Exodus, and the part called Deuteronomy. And each time, right after the Ten Commandments, come explanations of how they apply to everyday life.

A commandment and its explanations

For instance, there is the Commandment, "Thou shalt not covet."

A Jew might ask, "What shall I not covet?" And so the Bible tells him, right afterward, "Thou shalt not covet thy neighbor's house; thou shalt not covet thy neighbor's wife, nor his manservant, nor his maidservant, nor his ox, nor his donkey, nor anything that is thy neighbor's."

But some man in those days, just like someone you may know today, could have said, "Exactly what is my neighbor? Is everybody my neighbor? If I happen to find a donkey wandering on a road, doesn't it belong to me? Suppose it's not even my neighbor's donkey, but that it belonged to my enemy?"

The answer was given him, just a little further in the Bible, "If thou meet thine enemy's ox or his donkey gone astray, thou shalt surely bring it back to him again."

So we see that the Torah not only gave us the main rules, but gave us a picture of the way of life that grew around those rules. The Ten Commandments were the main statements and for each one, many rules had to be written. And even today, we have to keep on interpreting those rules to fit them to our own lives.

A free people needs laws

You know the Ten Commandments already. And you know how Moses wrote them down on tablets of stone, after he heard God speaking to him on Mount Sinai. The people of Israel needed laws because they had just escaped from slavery in Egypt. When they were slaves, they had had no rights. Now they had to learn to live together as a free people, with their rights and duties. They needed the Law of God to guide them. Therefore the first Commandment was to know God.

A slave is forced to do as his master orders. But a free man can choose what he does, instead of doing only what his master chooses. Therefore, when the Jews were freed from slavery, Moses brought them the Law.

Three commandments about God and man

The first Commandment was to know and remember that *God is*. This is a command to do; it is a command to know.

The second Commandment is a don't. It is a command against worshipping false idols. Long before Moses, in the time of Abraham, the Jews discovered

"Thou shalt not covet"

that God is One. Now, when they escaped from slavery, this idea helped them in deciding on one law, and only one.

The third Commandment is again a don't. It says, "Thou shalt not take the name of the Lord in vain." For instance, someone may tell a lie and say, "I swear by God it is true!" So this Commandment tells us not to use God to do bad.

Obeying the Sabbath and honoring parents

The fourth Commandment is "Remember the Sabbath Day, to keep it holy." This is a commandment to do. Do make one day of the week, the Sabbath, a day of rest, a day when you celebrate the goodness and beauty of life. From this you see that part of the Jewish way of life has always been to love life and live with joy.

The fifth Commandment is a do. It says, "Honor thy father and thy mother," and we know that this has always been with us in our way of life. It is not only about your father and mother, but about your grandparents and great grandparents and all your ancestors. It is a commandment to honor your whole history as a Jew, and be proud.

The first five Commandments, you see, all deal with a part of creation that is greater than ourselves. They deal with God, and with holiness, and with our parents and our ancestors.

Five don't's to guide mankind

Now come the second group of commandments, dealing with our life around us. The second group contains the great

I am the Lord thy God

Thou shalt have no other gods before me

Thou shalt not take the name of the Lord in vain

Remember the Sabbath day, to keep it holy

Honor thy father and thy mother

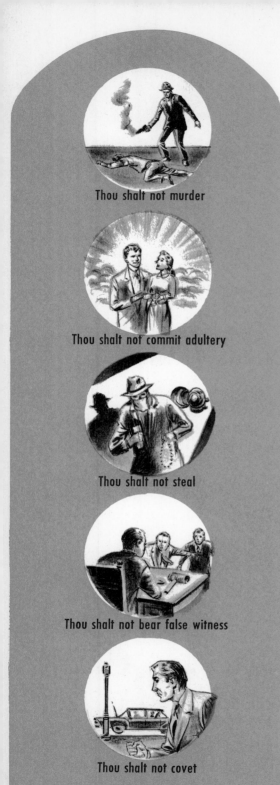

Thou shalt not murder

Thou shalt not commit adultery

Thou shalt not steal

Thou shalt not bear false witness

Thou shalt not covet

do nots. These make up the simplest and best code of law that mankind knows, because every child can understand and remember them.

The great do nots begin with the sixth Commandment which says "Thou shalt not murder." The seventh Commandment is "Thou shalt not commit adultery," which means that husband and wife should be true to each other. The eighth Commandment is "Thou shalt not steal." The ninth Commandment is "Thou shalt not bear false witness." To bear false witness means to lie, or gossip about others, or to accuse them of things they have not done.

The tenth Commandment, the last of the great do nots, is "Thou shalt not covet." Do not want things that belong to someone else; do not be envious or jealous, for this will only make you unhappy, and may cause you to steal or kill or do some other great wrong.

Laws to carry out the Commandments

In the Bible, the list of Commandments is followed at once by laws that help carry them out. "Now these are the ordinances," it says right after the Commandments. Then come many rules dealing with the fair treatment of servants, with planting and reaping, with hospitality to strangers, with everything that happens in daily life.

Elsewhere in the Bible, there are rules about paying people their wages as soon as they finish their work, and rules about feeding the poor and caring for the blind and respecting old age. And there is the great rule, "And thou shalt love thy neighbor as thyself."

37

In Canaan, the Jews settled down and became farm~

The Torah tells of the beginnings

The Torah tells us the day-by-day laws in the days of Moses, after he gave the Jews God's Ten Commandments. But besides our laws, the story of our people tells us much about our way of life. That, too, is in the Torah.

If you ask yourself, "Who am I? What am I? Where do I come from?" the answer is in the history of your people. If you were a child in the days of Moses and you asked these questions, your father or your grandfather would recite to you the story of your ancestors. He would tell of Abraham, the wanderer, and of his son Isaac, and his grandson Jacob, and his great grandson Joseph. Joseph became prime minister to the Pharoah of Egypt, and brought the whole tribe of Jews to Egypt.

He would tell how in Egypt, after many years, times became bad for the Jews and they were made slaves. And he would tell that the Jews left Egypt to go back to the old land of their ancestor Abraham, where they could again have a Jewish way of life.

But even when the Jews went back from Egypt, they did not go back exactly to their old way of life.

In the old days of Abraham, they had been wandering herdsmen, a tribal family with the wise old man as their chieftain. Now, coming out of Egypt, the Jews were a nation made up of many tribes and families. And so, instead of having a single patriarch as judge of right and wrong, they had a book of laws, which Moses gave them.

After they came into Canaan, instead of taking up the way of life of Abraham, as herdsmen moving about with their flocks, many of them settled in towns and villages. They became farmers. They planted vineyards and fruit trees that took many years to grow. They had homes for their families instead of tents.

The Temple in Jerusalem

Instead of a stone altar, where Abraham offered up prayers for the whole family tribe, the Jews built a Temple in Jerusalem. Instead of carrying the tablets of the Law in an Ark and keeping them under a tent, they built a Holy of Holies inside the Temple where the Ark was placed. They had settled down.

This did not happen all at once, but took a long time. Their settled way of life grew from the time of Joshua until the time of King Solomon. And when there was any question that could not be answered by the Torah laws, they went to the judges to be judged, and sometimes they asked the King.

When King Solomon died, the country was divided. Many years later, the Babylonians came and invaded Judea and destroyed the Temple in Jerusalem. They took many jews away from Judea to Babylonia.

Carrying the Torah to other lands

We know that the Jews once again carried their Torah laws with them, to Babylonia. And there they made more and more copies of the Torah, so that they were able to keep their laws and their way of life, even without the Temple.

That was the first proof that a people can keep their laws and customs, even when they are driven away from home. Still, in the new land many problems arose that could not be exactly explained by the laws in the Torah, and so there had to be new explanations of these laws to fit the new conditions of life.

The scribes and priests made these explanations as the cases came up, just as judges in our courts today will make decisions in each case, showing how the general law is to be used.

Torah links old ways and new ways

For laws have to deal with life as it is lived from day to day. But these laws are based on general principles which go far back, and which still guide our lives because they show us how our day-to-day laws must be made. Laws about stealing cars are not very different from laws about taking your neighbor's donkey.

So we see how our present way of life is linked to those ancient ways of life, how it was the books of the Torah that kept that link for us. Now we shall see how other books came to be written, and treasured by our people, to make further links in the chain of Jewish ideas that comes down to our own day.

THINKING ABOUT WHAT YOU HAVE LEARNED

1. The "Don't's" of the Commandments are a guide to living according to the highest ideals of Judaism. Can you make up some Don't's that would make your school class better?

QUESTIONS TO ASK YOUR PARENTS

1. What does this chapter mean when it says that slaves do not need laws but that free men do?
2. Why do we say that the Torah is a link between the earliest Jews and ourselves? 39

CHAPTER V

The Jewish Way of Life grows with the Talmud

American rules in the Constitution

You remember that when the American colonists started the United States of America, the first thing they did was to write down their rules. They called the main rules the Constitution.

But almost before they had finished writing the Constitution, they had to add to it, because of problems they hadn't thought of. So they called the next part the Bill of Rights. And after that came other amendments. And then came laws made by the Congress, and laws made by each state and each city.

And as new times came, and there were new inventions and changes in the American way of life, there were new laws. For instance, after the automobile was invented there had to be laws against speeding. But none of these new laws could go against any of the rights granted by the Constitution.

Now, long before America was started, something like this had happened to the Jewish people and their Torah. The Torah was not exactly like a modern Constitution, because constitutions are made by men, and the Torah was the word of God. It held the laws for the religious life of the Jews. It also had laws for the everyday life of the Jewish people, for in those days the laws of worship and the laws of everyday life were not separated.

The wisest of the rabbis knew the whole Torah by heart, and said that every problem could be explained by the Torah if you knew the meaning of each word and the meaning behind each word. So if a difficult problem arose, and a wise rabbi gave a good explanation, his explanation would be passed all over the country and talked about and used as an example, until it became a part of the law.

An example: care of a drowning animal

Here is an example. As Sabbath is a day of rest, what should a pious Jew do if, on a Sabbath, an animal fell into the water and could not get out?

One rabbi said, "If an animal has fallen into the water, a Jew may bring some pillows to place beneath it, so that it can come up on the ground." Another rabbi said, "If an animal has fallen into the water, we shall provide it with fodder, where it is, so that it shall not die. Then, after the Sabbath, it can be brought out onto the ground."

Pious Jews argued the decision. Some said if you could feed the animal and keep him alive, then it was wrong to bring pillows that would sink in the water. Because there is another rule that says it is wrong to spoil a useful thing. And to sink pillows in the water spoils them, so they can't be used again.

The rabbis decided that both decisions came from the word of God in the Torah, which says you shall save life. But preventing pain to an animal, such as the pain of hunger, is a command of the Torah. And it is a higher command than the rule about saving the usefulness of a thing, which was a rule made by rabbis. So the right thing to do if an animal fell into the water was to feed him, and to bring him out of the water after the Sabbath.

How the Bible grew

As years went on, the rabbis had to remember not only the Torah, but hundreds of cases and explanations for every law in the Torah. Later, after the destruction of the Temple in 70 C.E., more cases came up. These wise rulings were called the Oral Law, because they were not yet written down. Many rabbis said it was not a good idea to write down the Oral Law, because it would then be considered as important as the holy words of the Bible. But finally

An animal in danger on the Sabbath

41

there were too many oral examples to remember.

How the Talmud was written

Then there came another danger that the laws of the Jewish way of life might be lost. For many Jews were driven across the sea by the Romans, and others escaped to Babylonia and Egypt and to different lands. As the Jews were scattered, it became necessary for them to have their laws written down.

A large number of Jews were still living in Babylonia, for not all of the Jewish families had come back to Jerusalem, just as today not all of the Jewish families go back to live in Israel. And in Babylonia, too, there were academies of Jewish learning.

Both in Babylonia and Palestine, the academies of rabbis began to write down the laws and the wisdom and the stories that explained the Torah. Judah Hanasi put them together to make the Mishnah. Then for almost three hun-

The Babylonian exile

dred years, hundreds of rabbis and scholars continued to discuss and add to these writings. That is how the Talmud was written.

Halachah and Agada

There were two kinds of writing in the Talmud. One kind was made of rules, such as the rules about the animal who fell into the water. These rules were like cases decided by a judge in a law court today.

Suppose there is a case in a law court about two cars that bumped into each other just as the traffic light was changing. Which car had the right of way? Each side will try to show that the law is in its favor, and then the judge will decide. In the same way, in olden times, if two men came with a dispute, the rabbi or court would decide. If the case was complicated, and the Torah law didn't tell exactly what to do, they would try to remember what some other rabbi had done in a similar case. And so the rabbi's decision would be added to make the law more clear.

All these decisions and all these laws, together were called the *Halachah*. There were laws about marriage and divorce and debts, and about what kinds of seeds to plant in the fields and when to plant them, as well as laws about worship.

But then there was a second kind of writing in the Talmud. When a rabbi wanted to make it easy for the people to understand a law, he might invent a little story that could serve as an example. These stories are called *Agada*. Sometimes they were told about great

Abraham Lincoln tells a story in court

heroes like David. Sometimes they were stories about ordinary people.

In modern times, Abraham Lincoln used the same method. We have wonderful tales told by Abraham Lincoln when he was a lawyer, because the stories were easier to understand than the dry words of the law.

The Agada is not a new idea, for we know that tales are used to teach a moral. For instance, the tale was told that when God created Adam, the father of all men, he took dust from lands all over the world. He took a little earth from the four corners of the earth. In that way, no people could say, "We are greater than our neighbor, for Adam was born here."

43

And so, though there already is a Torah law that says, "And thou shalt love thy neighbor as thyself," we have also an Agada to show us the meaning of that rule.

Both rules and stories

For hundreds of years, the Jews living in Palestine and Babylonia put their rules and their story-lessons together into the Talmud. And when we study the Talmud today, we can see what their way of life was like in those times.

But the Jews scattered to far places and to smaller communities where they did not have access to the Talmud, for printing had not yet been invented and a vast work like the Talmud took years to copy. The ordinary Jew had many questions about his Jewish way of life. In some places, there were Jewish communities without a rabbi. These scattered Jews were not even sure which were the proper prayers to say on the Sabbath. We shall see what they did to preserve their Jewish way of life.

THINKING ABOUT WHAT YOU HAVE LEARNED

1. The Bible says that you should not work on the Sabbath nor cause anyone else to work. Does this mean that you should not buy a book on Saturday?
2. Why did God make only one man to begin with? So that no man can say, "I am better than any other," for we are all descended from Adam. This is an Agada. Can you think of another one?

QUESTIONS TO ASK YOUR PARENTS

1. How do we Americans find answers to our questions about law and government?
2. The Talmud often describes both sides of an argument before giving a decision. Why is this important in a book of laws?

CHAPTER VI

The Jewish Way of Life grows for a thousand more years

Do you knew that the newspapers of today keep up a custom that the Jews started long long ago? It is the custom of giving answers to problems that are sent in a letter.

Questions to a newspaper

In almost every newspaper you will find a column in which an expert answers letters. The column may be called "Your Health," or "The Worry Clinic," or "Advice to the Lovelorn."

It may be a column of advice about taking care of children. A mother may write in and ask, "I have two children, and the big one is jealous of the little one. What shall I do?" A doctor or a psychologist may answer the mother's letter; then other mothers who have the same problem can be helped by the same answer.

The custom of question-and-answer letters goes back hundreds of years to the time when the Jews were scattered from their homeland. When a small number of Jews went to live in Spain, for instance, they wrote to the rabbis in Babylonia, asking what prayers were the best to read during Sabbath services. The answer that came from the great Rab Amram contained a list of prayers, and formed the beginning of the prayer-book we use today.

Responsa

Such answers were called Responsa, and the Responsa became important. For, even after all the laws had been collected in the Talmud, there were still new questions that were not exactly answered in the Talmud. If a rabbi wrote a good Responsum on such a question, his answer would be copied and handed around, so that it became an addition to the law.

In those early times there was no system for sending mail. A Jew who lived in Spain and wanted to ask a question of a rabbi in Babylonia would try to find someone travelling in that general direction. He might find a merchant going as far as Alexandria. The merchant would carry the letter with him, and look for someone going further, 45

Was Reuben responsible for the money he lost?

perhaps to Jerusalem. So the letter would pass through several hands and take maybe a year to get to Babylonia. And the Responsum might take a year to get back.

Even today, though we have airmail letters and telegrams, people will still give messages to friends who are travelling to far places. You may notice your parents saying, "Please take a message for me," when they have a friend going to Israel.

46 And just as the habit of sending mes-

sages through travellers is kept up, so is the habit of asking questions from experts. Jews who go into the army, for example, may read booklets of Responsa by great rabbis, on the question of fighting in a war.

A question about a highway robbery

In the old days, the rabbis settled many questions that would today be settled by courts of law. For instance, here is a Responsum that was found among some very ancient documents in Cairo, Egypt.

It is a question that was asked perhaps a thousand years ago. It deals with highway robbery, yet we might be puzzled by what is right and what is wrong in such a case, even today.

The Responsum is by a great rabbi and the question is from a man named Reuben who travelled in a caravan to Egypt. His friend Simeon had given him fifteen dinars, to buy merchandise. But Reuben wrote, "Brigands came and captured the entire caravan. I was stripped to the skin and they prepared to slaughter me. I thought, 'I am unable to save anything in my possession from their hands. It is better therefore if I tell them I have money with me, and they may spare my life.' I told them I had got money with me, fifteen dinars. I took them to the box, opened it, took Simeon's fifteen dinars and gave it to them and saved myself thus. I am ready to pay Simeon half the money because of my friendship."

Was it a sin to follow a false Messiah?

DISPERSAL OF THE JEWS AFTER THE ROMAN CONQUEST

Many Jews had been living in other countries before the destruction of the Temple at Jerusalem in 70 C.E., but that year marked the end of Judea as the national center of Jewry and the beginning of the Diaspora, or dispersion, which existed until this century.

ENGLAND
Jews were restricted to trade, medicine and money-lending. Conditions grew worse until they were expelled entirely in 1290.

GERMANY
Jews lived in relative freedom until the oppressions of the Crusades and the Black Death.

POLAND received many Jews seeking to escape from the oppressions of the Crusades and the Black Death, as well as survivors of the Jewish kingdom of Khazaria.

RUSSIA

KHAZARIA

FRANCE
Jews were able to enter many fields of work, and under Charlemagne enjoyed great religious freedom. Conditions then worsened until the Jews were expelled from northern France in 1306.

BOHEMIA

SPAIN
Jewish culture flourished from about 700 to 1100. Then came Arab wars, the Inquisition, and the expulsion of the Jews in 1492.

ITALY
For many years, Jews led fairly free lives, becoming jewelers, carpenters, smiths, weavers, etc.

GREECE

TURKEY

JUDEA

BABYLONIA
Jews continued to live and flourish after 70 C. Learning continued for many centuries at the academies of Sura, Pumpeditha and Nehard

But Simeon complained, "This man has saved himself through my money; therefore he is obliged to pay it all back."

The Responsum said, "Reuben was right in saying that the bandits would have taken the money in any case. If witnesses confirm the narrative, he is free. If he has no witnesses, he shall make an oath that the highwaymen would have seized the dinars, even if they had killed him. If Simeon accepts the half of the money offered by Reuben as a compromise, Reuben is released from his obligation."

A question about a false Messiah

Other letters dealt with spiritual matters instead of everyday matters. For instance, the Jews longed for the Messiah who would lead them back to the Holy Land. And from time to time appeared a false Messiah, a man who proclaimed himself the Messiah. And many

48

Jews would follow the false Messiah and give him money, and obey his commands.

Was it a sin for a Jew to follow a false Messiah? Such questions were asked, and the scholar would say that the followers of a false Messiah should be forgiven their mistake, because it was a mistake made out of goodness, out of their longing for the true Messiah to appear. In our own lives we often hear of people following a bad leader, called a "false Messiah," and we wonder if they are to blame.

Thus you see that the great rabbis pondered problems that come right into our own lives. Hai Gaon, a rabbi of Babylonia, is said to have received a thousand question-letters in his lifetime. Rabbi Meir of Rothenberg, some centuries later in Germany, is said to have answered fifteen hundred letters, and Rabbi Solomon Ibn Adret is said to have answered three thousand.

Answer for every hour of the day

From these Responsa, we can tell what questions the Jews worried about, and therefore we can learn a good deal about how they lived, through those centuries of history. And there are other records of how they lived. The list of prayers for the Sabbath was only the beginning of the many lists which Jews used. After a time there was a list of answers that told each Jew exactly what he had to do day and night.

Did you ever follow a printed schedule? It might be a list made in a camp. It says after rising, you must wash and dress. It tells you that after lunch, you must rest or write letters home.

Suppose one day you would like to go for a walk instead of going to arts and crafts class. You have to find out whether the rules say it is all right. And you have to find out what the punishment might be if you break the rules.

Now, in a simple way, this can give you an idea of how pious Jews were guided in their everyday life. Of course you must not think of the Jewish way of life in olden times, as something like going to camp. But it is hard to find something in your own life that will make you understand what the lives of pious Jews were like. Because the program they lived by was not simply a program of convenience. They thought of it as God's program. Every rule, every action was directed by their religion.

Rules for walking and eating

Suppose you were a Jew living in that old world. You would know it was forbidden to travel on Sabbath. How far could you walk, without calling it travelling? Could you walk in your own garden? And to the synagogue? A hundred yards? Two hundred yards? The exact distance was written in the rules.

The pious Jew needed a list, or code, of foods that were kosher to eat. There were new questions about food every time the Jews moved on to a new country. After America was discovered, for example, there were foods that people had never known before. There was corn on the cob. There were tomatoes. And also, there was such a thing as tobacco. Was there a blessing to say before smoking tobacco? The Bible did not

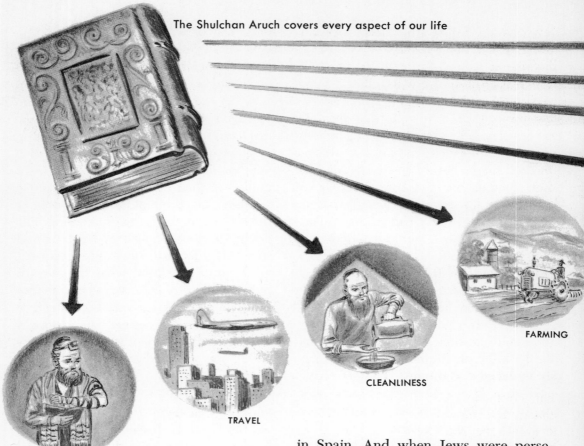

The Shulchan Aruch covers every aspect of our life

PRIVATE PRAYER

TRAVEL

CLEANLINESS

FARMING

speak of it. The Talmud did not speak of it. What did the Responsa say?

A directory of all the rules

In order to make things easier for the average Jew, the rabbis tried to make directories of all the rules. Maimonides wrote such a book which he called the "Mishneh Torah." But the most famous of these directories, or codes, was written by another Spanish Jew, Rabbi Joseph Caro. He was born about the time when Columbus discovered America, the time when there was an Inquisition in Spain. And when Jews were persecuted and driven out of that country, Rabbi Caro moved from Spain to Turkey.

He was worried because in moving about from one country to another, the Jews could not always carry their books. And also, many Jews became scattered. So more than ever they needed a simple code of their laws. For twenty years he worked, trying to bring the rules of the vast Talmud, and of the Responsa, into a practical code. And he named this code the *Shulchan Aruch*, which means "the set table." Thus, each regulation in the life of the Jew had its proper place.

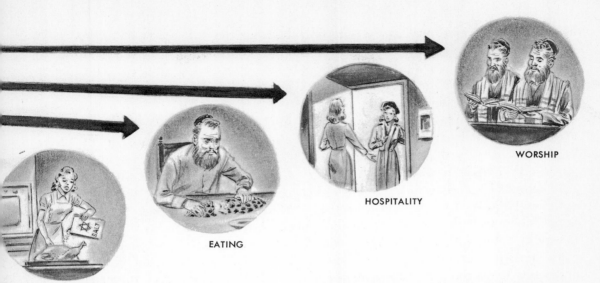

COOKING

EATING

HOSPITALITY

WORSHIP

Six hundred and thirteen rules

This code came out in 1567. It did not change the rules of life for the Jews but it made the rules easier to find, and therefore more and more Jews began to live in the same way, from morning through night. Not only was a Jew's daily life arranged, but he was given the rules for the festivals, the laws about planting and about property and even about visiting the sick.

In the "Table" there were 613 items which a Jew should observe. Jews in those days liked to find meanings in numbers. So out of the 613 regulations they counted 365 things *not to do*, the same number as there are days in the year. If you subtract 365 from 613, that leaves 248, and these were the things a good Jew should do. And this number also was easy to remember, for they thought there were 248 bones in the body. Now, as we have a habit of counting on our fingers; so in that way they could count off the "do's" on Rabbi Caro's list!

Though several other rabbis wrote rule books, the "Table" of Rabbi Joseph Caro was accepted by the Jewish people as the most useful. For hundreds of years, the Jews lived by Rabbi Caro's Shulchan Aruch. This is one reason their way of life was so clear and exact, even though they were scattered in many countries.

Laws about washing hands

Here is an example from the Shulchan Aruch, showing how the rules were explained. It is from the chapter on "Laws Relating to the Washing of the Hands in the Morning."

"Because a man rising from his bed is like a new creature in so far as the service of the Creator is concerned, blessed be He, it is incumbent upon him to purify himself and wash his 51 hands out of a vessel just as the priest was accustomed to purify his hands daily out of the washbasin prior to his services in the Temple . . . One is not permitted to walk four cubits without having his hands washed, except in extreme cases of necessity."

The Jew is even told exactly how to wash his hands: "In the morning the hands are to be washed in the following manner: He takes the vessel in his right hand and puts it in the left; thereupon he spills water with the left upon the right, and then he takes it in the right and spills it on the left, repeating this performance three times. . . . One must wash his face in honor of his Creator; because it is said: 'For in the image of God hath he made the man' (Gen. IX, 6). He must also rinse his mouth of saliva, because he has to make mention of the great Name in purity and cleanliness. . . ."

"Before his morning hand-washing he must not touch his mouth, nor his eyes, nor his nose, nor any kind of food . . .

because the evil spirit that rests upon the hands before washing is injurious to such places and things." This too is a rule of purity and cleanliness.

Rules kept up the way of life

Even today there are many Jews throughout the world who guide their lives day by day, hour after hour, according to the 613 do's and don't's of the Shulchan Aruch. In the old days, when the Jews were driven out of Spain and other countries where they were persecuted, and wandered to the far regions like Poland and Russia, they could keep their way of life by observing all these rules.

And we shall see how their way of life flourished in these olden times when Jews were allowed to live only in certain countries, and in certain parts of the cities called ghettoes. Because they lived close together, and were kept apart from the other people of those lands, the Jewish way of life had a character of its own.

THINKING ABOUT WHAT YOU HAVE LEARNED

1. Rabbis today still write Responsa (answers) to questions about Jewish law and how it would answer their own problems. Your class may want to ask your rabbi to tell about some of the questions people ask him. Would you also have a question for him?

2. If the case of the man in the highway robbery came to trial, whose lawyer would you rather be? Why?

QUESTIONS TO ASK YOUR PARENTS

1. The 613 rules of the Shulchan Aruch are called "mitzvoth," sometimes translated as "commandments." Ask your parents how they would translate mitzvoth, especially about such things as rules for washing hands and eating.

2. Did the old Jewish laws about washing and being clean help keep the Jewish people alive during their long history?

The Jewish
Way of Life
in the Ghetto

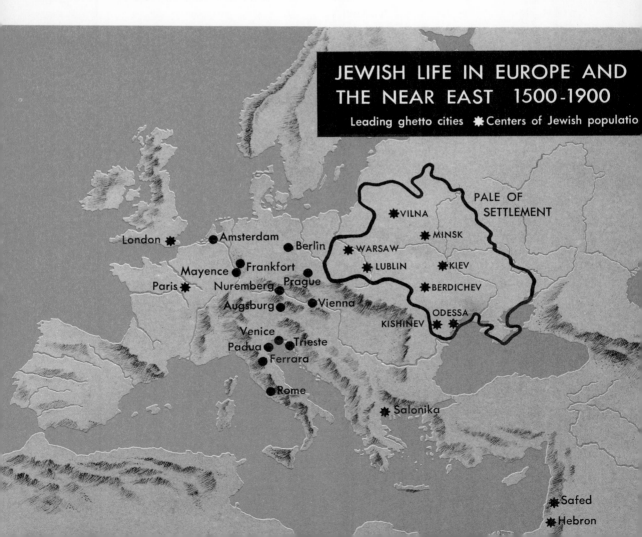

**JEWISH LIFE IN EUROPE AND
THE NEAR EAST 1500-1900**
Leading ghetto cities ✴ Centers of Jewish populatio

PALE OF
SETTLEMENT

✴VILNA

✴ MINSK

London ✴
● Amsterdam
● Berlin
✴ WARSAW
Mayence ● ● Frankfort
✴ LUBLIN   ✴ KIEV
Paris ✴   Nuremberg ● ● Prague
✴ BERDICHEV
Augsburg ● ● Vienna
✴ ODESSA
KISHINEV ✴
Venice ●
Padua ● ● Trieste
Ferrara ●

Rome ●
✴ Salonika

✴ Safed

✴ Hebron

CHAPTER VII

Life inside the Ghetto

Not long ago, in fact in the time of our great-grandfathers, the Jewish way of life was much the same for most Jews, from day to day, because they lived by the "Table," or the Shulchan Aruch. And also, because in many places the Jews had walls around them.

These were the walls of the ghetto. The ghetto was the only place where Jews were allowed to live. Sometimes it was a special part of a city, and sometimes it was an entire town only for Jews. Sometimes the ghetto had a gate that would be locked at night.

The Ghetto in Venice

Perhaps the very earliest ghetto was in the city of Venice, in Italy. As you know, Venice is a beautiful city with canals instead of streets, and with bridges over the canals. One of these bridges had little shops and houses on top of it, and these were Jewish shops. The bridge led into the Jewish part of town, and Jews were not allowed to live in any other part of town. During the day, they could go and do business in other parts of the city of Venice, but at night they had to stay in their own neighborhood, which was called a ghetto.

There were several reasons for this separation. Jews were foreigners in Venice, and their religion was different from the religion of the Italians, who were Christians. In those days, people were very superstitious, and afraid of foreigners, and there was fear and hatred of anyone with strange customs. So the Jews were locked up in a small part of the city where they could be watched. Sometimes, too, it was a protection for them to live close together.

Ghettos in the countries of Europe

Ghettos were found not only in Venice but in other countries where Jews were sent to live. Years before they had wandered up into Europe from the seacoasts of Italy and France; and they went to live in Germany, in towns along the Rhine River. And from Germany they wandered up north, into Poland and into Russia. In these countries, too, special laws were made about where the Jews could live, and what they could do for a living.

In most of these countries, Jews were not allowed to own land, so they could not become farmers. They had to be traders, and shop keepers, and craftsmen, living in their own little communities. Even if there was no real wall around them, there was still a wall of special laws which made them live quite separately from the other people in those countries.

Yiddish: the language of the people

The Jews even had their own languages. In the ghettos of Greece and Turkey they spoke a language called Ladino. In Poland and in Russia and in Roumania and in Hungary, they kept on speaking Jewish, or Yiddish as it was called, among themselves. They had their own newspapers and books in the Yiddish language.

In America, everybody speaks the same language, English. When people come to live in America, they learn to

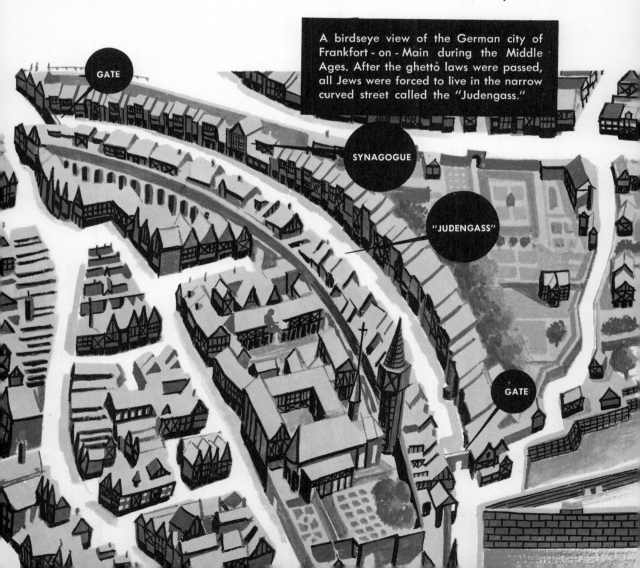

GATE

A birdseye view of the German city of Frankfort - on - Main during the Middle Ages. After the ghetto laws were passed, all Jews were forced to live in the narrow curved street called the "Judengass."

SYNAGOGUE

"JUDENGASS"

GATE

speak English. But when they first come, they speak the language of the old country, especially among themselves. And of course if a group of newcomers got closed off into their own town, like a ghetto, they would keep on speaking their own language among themselves, because it would be easier.

That was what happened to the Jews in the old days in the old country. What was that language known as "Yiddish?" Was it the language Jews had always had, from the time of Moses? No, that language was Hebrew. Then where did the Jews get this other language? Did they make it up?

Does it sound like any other language? There is a clue. It sounds like German. In fact, it has mostly the same words as German. But it also has many Hebrew words. This gives us the answer.

When you are trying to learn a new language, and you still don't know enough words to be able to say everything you want to say, what do you do? You mix in a word from your old language whenever you get stuck. Sometimes that old word is a very good word. Like the word "kibbitzer." This is a Yiddish word that Jews kept on using after they came to this country and learned English, because there was no English word that meant exactly the same thing. So pretty soon, "kibbitzer" began to be used by everybody. Other

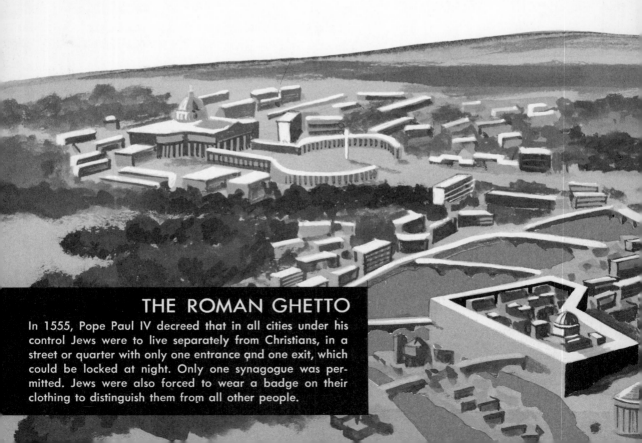

THE ROMAN GHETTO

In 1555, Pope Paul IV decreed that in all cities under his control Jews were to live separately from Christians, in a street or quarter with only one entrance and one exit, which could be locked at night. Only one synagogue was permitted. Jews were also forced to wear a badge on their clothing to distinguish them from all other people.

Americans took it up, and it became part of the American language. That is how languages grow and change.

Yiddish is German plus Hebrew

And back there centuries ago when some Jews went to live in Germany, they learned and spoke the German language, but mixed in many Hebrew words. After a few hundred years the Jews had bad times in Germany. Even long before the days of the Nazis, they were persecuted by Germans, and large numbers of Jews fled to Poland. But by then, German was their language, and they kept on talking the German language among themselves, even in Poland.

One reason was the way they lived in Poland. In those days, in Poland and in Russia, the land was owned by noblemen. Each landlord owned very large estates, and had entire towns of peasants working for him. As the Jews did not own any land, and were not peasants, they could only become traders and also craftsmen, furriers, tailors, carpenters.

And as they had to live near each other to practice their religion, they gathered together in small communities. They kept among themselves, and they kept on talking and writing in the language they already knew, the language they had brought from Germany. As their children grew, they learned this

The Roman Ghetto was located on the banks of the Tiber River, which often flooded homes and destroyed property.

house, and for newspapers, and for storybooks. Hebrew was the Sabbath language for worship and for scholars.

The reason more Jews didn't learn Polish was that they lived in small towns and traded among themselves, except for the few rich and important Jews of each village, who were tax collectors for the Polish noblemen, or those who kept the village inn or the village store. Those Jews did learn Polish.

Jews lived in a special way

You do not live in a ghetto. You may live in a street or neighborhood where many Jews live, but this is not because of a law forcing Jews to do so. Jews, like everyone else, have a right to live wherever they please. There is no wall and no gate that is closed at night.

You speak the same language as your non-Jewish neighbors, and you go to the same schools, read the same magazines and books, and see the same movies. You wear the same clothes. Your parents pay the same taxes and vote in the same elections.

Now, imagine how it was in the Jewish towns in Poland and those other countries. The Jews had to pay special taxes, and they could not vote, even for a long time after other people won citizen's rights.

The Jews dressed in a special way, and you can still see some Jews in our large cities who keep this old-style form of dress and who allow their ear-curls to grow, because it is a part of the rules they believe in.

Most Jews of the ghetto read only their own books. They had their own

German-sounding language.

There were no public schools for the Jews, indeed only the sons of the noblemen had teachers, and very few other children went to school. And even later, when the peasants won more rights in those countries, and schools were established, only a few seats were allowed for the Jewish children.

So the Jews had their own schools, and these were almost all religious schools, because the boys studied the Torah. They studied it in Hebrew, so many Hebrew words were mixed in with the Yiddish words that were used in the ghettos and in the towns, in daily life, and in newspapers and books. That was how Yiddish grew to be a language all by itself. It had a flavor and expressions all its own.

But instead of being written the same way German was written, it was written in the Hebrew alphabet, so that while it sounded something like German, it looked like Hebrew.

You could say that the Jews had a Sabbath language and a weekday language. Yiddish was the weekday language, for everyday talk around the

58

schools, and if a boy was a bright scholar he left home to go to a religious college or yeshiva.

The Jews took care not only of their own schools, but of everything in the community. If there was a quarrel among Jews, they had their own rabbinical court for settling the argument, and tried to stay out of the civil court.

Since they lived this way for generations, with Yiddish as their main language, Jews soon had their own newspapers and magazines in Yiddish, and their own writers, many of whom became famous. Today we still read many of these writers in English translations, writers like Sholom Aleichem and Mendele Mocher S'forim. And so we get stories and pictures in our minds of the way of life of the Jews of that time.

What Jews did for a living

What did those Jews do for a living? They did all the village things; they were shoemakers and tailors and bakers. They sold things in the marketplace to farmers who came from the countryside. They bought and sold cattle and horses. Often the village innkeeper was a Jew. And the Jews became bookkeepers and managers on the large estates of the Polish noblemen. They would arrange for the sale of lumber from the forests. And some would work as tax collectors.

When they collected taxes from Jews for the nobleman, who was called a "paritz," they would at the same time collect a Jewish community tax, for keeping up the synagogue and the school and for helping the poor.

A Jewish innkeeper in Eastern Europe

A tablecloth for Rabbi Caro's "Table"

The Polish Jews of that time were extremely pious, and of course they were very strict about the laws of Kashruth and other regulations. Travelers who had learned about Rabbi Joseph Caro's "Table," the Shulchan Aruch, brought copies of this useful rulebook to the Jews of Poland. They saw that their own customs were a little bit different from the regulations that Rabbi Caro had put into his code for the Sefardic Jews.

So an extra part was added to "The Set Table." This was called the "Mapah," or the Tablecloth, and it was the work of Rabbi Moses Isserles who died in 1572. And this became the code for Jewish life in what many American Jews speak of as "the old country."

What we owe to this Jewish way of life

Those of our people who came from Poland and Russia and neighboring lands, brought this way of life with them to America. In America, it gradually changed. Yet many of the customs in our own way of life today we owe to their ways. Many of the words in our language we owe to Yiddish. Many of the tasty dishes of which we are fond we owe to the Jewish cookery of those lands. And many of the deeper ideas in our lives we owe to the Jews of the old country.

One of these ideas is the love of learning, which had been a rule and a tradition among the Jews from far back in Biblical times, but which the Jews of Europe made even stronger and more universal than ever before.

THINKING ABOUT WHAT YOU HAVE LEARNED

1. While the ghetto was a wall which kept Jews inside a certain area of the city, did it have any advantages for the Jews of this period?
2. Why did Yiddish develop as the language of the Polish Jewish ghetto?

QUESTIONS TO ASK YOUR PARENTS

1. Today the word ghetto is used for any neighborhood in which any people are forced to live. Are there such neighborhoods in your city?
2. How are Jewish community institutions supported today, compared with the way they were supported by Jews in the European ghettos?

An early printing press

CHAPTER VIII

Study as a Way of Life

Today, parents are proud of many things in their children. They are proud when a child gets along well with others, and is elected to office in a club or in class. They are proud when a child is very good in sports and gets on a team. They are proud of course when a child is talented in music or art or writing or dancing or acting. But they are proudest of all when a child is bright in his class studies.

Pride in the glory of a bright student

This pride comes from the old Jewish tradition of having pride in the scholar. In the old Jewish way of life, nothing counted so much as the glory of a bright student. There were no star athletes in the old days in Eastern Europe. And for many years, up to the modern time called the Enlightenment, there was only one subject that was studied: It was the Torah. All knowledge and all wisdom was said to be in the Bible, the Talmud, and other Jewish religious works. This was the Jewish

law, and it was history too, and in many ways it was science.

Study was a commandment

To the Jews, study was a commandment. For in the Bible, right after the Sh'ma, "Hear, O Israel, the Lord Our God, the Lord Is One," there is a commandment to teach the Law of God to our children. "And these words, which I command thee this day, shall be upon thy heart. And thou shalt teach them diligently to thy children . . ."

This commandment is so important that it is repeated by the Jews at almost every religious service.

Greatest heroes were scholars and wise men

From the time of Moses, the Jews always honored their scribes and scholars and rabbis. Their greatest heroes were scholars and wise men. David was a hero not only because he was a brave warrior who slew Goliath, but because he was a poet, and because he brought

61

back the Ark of the Covenant to Jerusalem. Ezra was a hero because he taught the Jews to have the Torah read out loud so that everyone could learn and understand it.

Rabbi Akiba was a great hero because of his wisdom and learning, and the warrior Bar Kochba respected him and sought his blessing. Out of the Middle Ages, the name we best remember in Jewish lore is the name of Maimonides, the great Spanish physician and scholar. Out of all the history of the Jews in Poland and Russia, it is not the men of wealth that we remember; it is the scholars and the writers and the great

rabbis whose names stand foremost in our history. The Gaon of Vilna was such a man.

Memorizing the Talmud

And in those days, Jewish children understood from their earliest years that glory came through study. There were brilliant Jewish children who could recite the whole Bible by heart, before they were Bar Mitzvah. A favorite story is told about sticking a needle through several pages of the Talmud. Perhaps it would pierce a dozen pages. After you told a bright student what word the needle went through on the first page,

In a House of Study

he could tell you, without looking, each word that the needle had pierced on each of the other eleven pages. For he had the Talmud pictured page by page in his mind.

As soon as a boy could learn to read, his family watched for signs of unusual scholarship. Especially was this true in poor families. For if a boy was an outstanding Talmud student, his fame would spread, and before he was thirteen he would be sought after as a son-in-law by the richest parents in the countryside.

The rich families would listen to matchmakers who went from one town to another, looking for the brightest students. For the greatest ornament that a rich family could have would be a famous talmudist for a son-in-law.

They would make a marriage contract while the boy and girl were still very young, and the young husband would be given a large marriage gift, or dowry, and be supported by the father-in-law, so that he could keep on with his studies, and bring fame and glory to the household and the town.

How poor students lived

Students who were not yet married would live near a famous rabbi, as part of his circle of students. How would they live? They would sleep on a bench in the study room, or perhaps in someone's attic. The poor students would be given "eating days" at the homes of the Jews of the town. Thus, a student might eat every Monday with the leather dealer, and every Tuesday with the lumber dealer, and every Wednesday with a tailor's family, and so on. Sometimes, one day would be missing, as the town itself might be poor. In that case, the student would fast on his missing day.

It was considered a great "mitzvah," or good deed, to provide an eating day for a student of the Torah, and poor families often would deprive themselves in order to help such scholars.

Many of the romantic stories of famous Yiddish writers like Peretz and Mendele Mocher S'forim are about students who fell in love with the daughters of their hosts, on their eating days. But they were very shy, for it was con-

sidered a temptation and something of a sin for a student of the holy books even to look at a woman.

The importance of scholars

We may wonder why the Jews of that time were so proud of having a talmudic scholar in the family. The answer is that the whole life of the people was held together by the scholars. The Torah was their law. The scholar was a kind of lawyer and judge and teacher and rabbi, all in one.

If a town had a scholar who was quick with his talmudic quotations, the people of the town would brag about him wherever they went. Sometimes there were matches of wits between students from different towns. A question about a Sabbath rule might be brought up, and then each scholar would quote the opinion of a great rabbi, and the one who could quote the most authoritative opinions would have the last word. It was a special kind of legalistic debate.

A town could become famous because of a rabbi

As the talmudist became older, he might become a teacher somewhere, or he might become a rabbi. People would come, asking him to settle disputes. Two merchants who might have a business dispute would agree, "Let the Gaon of Vilna settle it." And they would make a journey to his "court" to have the question settled. Thus, a whole town might become famous because of a wise rabbi.

In your home, parents may like to show off their children by having them sing

a song, or play a piece of music, or recite a poem. But in the old country, fathers would show off their sons, usually at the Sabbath table when there were guests, by having them recite from the Torah. And every Sabbath, the father would test his son by asking Torah questions to see what he had learned during the week. The women would listen, and the young girls would listen and watch with awe.

Special terms for students and scholars

There were special words for those who devoted themselves altogether to studying. Such a student was called a "mathmid."

Someone who knew the Talmud well was called a "Talmid hacham."

There were other special words for brilliant scholars. A very learned person was called a "lamdan," and a really gifted student was called an "ilui," which is like a child genius. An ilui who lived with great purity studying day and night, became a holy person and might then be called a "gaon."

Naturally, not all Jewish men could spend their entire lives in study, and not everyone was gifted with a good memory. But even merchants and other workers tried to keep up with their learning in their spare time. Groups of men would get together in the synagogue on certain evenings, and study the Talmud a few pages at a time.

You may know adults who go to evening classes or have study circles at home, studying Jewish history or the Hebrew language. Or they may study the great books, or they may go outside

A young scholar is examined on the Sabbath

the field of Jewish studies, and meet to read Shakespeare. All this is in the Jewish spirit of love for learning.

Celebrating the completion of a book

In the old country, when a Jewish study group completed a part of the Talmud, called a tractate, they would hold a little celebration, a "siyum." They might drink a toast and sing some songs. Then they would start on the next tractate at the same meeting, to show that learning is never ended. You will recognize that this is the same idea as in Simchath Torah. When the last portion of the Torah is reached, the first portion is begun at the very same service, to show that the study of the Torah never stops.

In the world of the ghetto, study continued to be a good deed in itself, a mitzvah, and to help others to study was also a mitzvah. Good deeds of this kind could be added up during a man's lifetime, to give a good Jew his "share of heaven."

But a way in which a Jew sampled his share of heaven right here on earth was in the old-fashioned Sabbath. We shall see what such a Sabbath was like.

THINKING ABOUT WHAT YOU HAVE LEARNED

1. In what ways did the Jews of the ghetto show their respect for learning?
2. What in the life of a Polish Jewish boy who spent all of his days studying would make up for his missing some of the things you enjoy?

QUESTIONS TO ASK YOUR PARENTS

1. Does your family have any heirlooms? Are they Sabbath utensils? What is the history of your family heirlooms?
2. Ask your parents to tell you about the adult education program in your congregation.

CHAPTER IX

A bit of Heaven on Earth

We know of Sabbath as the seventh day, which is a day of rest. We know that such a day is commanded in the Ten Commandments. So we understand that it must be important. But why did it need a whole Commandment? Did Jews really need one of the Ten Commandments for people to get a day off from work?

A day of rest made all men equal

Yes. In Biblical times, a regular day of rest was a strange new idea. And to give a regular day of rest to slaves was unheard of. So this Commandment was a very important new idea because it made all people, slaves and masters, equal in the sight of God. And if they were equal in regard to a Sabbath, they could be equal in other things.

A day for thoughts of higher things

But the seventh day, the Sabbath, was not merely a day off. It was a day set apart so that man could devote himself to spiritual things. Only on such a day, free from all care, could he think of

heaven and the universe and truth and justice, without tangling these thoughts with his selfish wishes in his workaday life.

Here in America, we live and work with other Americans who usually take Sunday off. But as more and more people have two days off each week, those Jews who wish to observe their traditional Sabbath can more easily do so.

From this Sunday-Sabbath question alone, we can see that our life is quite different from the way of life of the Jews in the old country villages. They strictly kept the traditional Sabbath as their day of rest. All their stores and shops were closed.

The Sabbath spirit in songs

But their day of rest was more than the "day off." It was more, even, than the day on which they said certain prayers in the synagogue. If we ever can come to feel what their Sabbath was truly like, in those times, then we will understand a Jewish way of life from which a beautiful melody still seems to rise to us.

And perhaps it is from the very songs of Sabbath that we can best understand what such a day was like. The Jews of that time sang Sabbath songs at their table, as many of us still do, and these songs were about Sabbath coming like a "bride" or a "queen."

Indeed, the weekly coming of Sabbath to the home was something like a wedding. A heavenly wedding, each week. It was also a day of worship in the home itself.

Sabbath joins the family in worship

When you think of religion, you think mostly of synagogues or temples, and of a whole congregation of people coming to worship together. But there are times when people want to pray all by themselves, and there are times when it is the family that is joined in a feeling of worship.

The Sabbath was a family time. And worship was not only a service. The Sabbath was joy and peace that came over

The large and handsome synagogue of Amsterdam, Holland. Until about 1800, this was the richest and most important Jewish community in western Europe. Synagogues in this part of the world, unlike the eastern European one seen on page 72, usually had a long prayer room, with the bimah near one end and the Ark at the other.

WOMEN'S BALCONY

ARK OF THE TORAH

BIMAH

the entire house. The Jewish word for resting on the Sabbath does not mean merely the rest that is an absence from work. The word is "m'nuchah," and that means peaceful enjoyment. The Sabbath was really a heavenly time, and the Jews of those days thought of each Sabbath as though it were a taste on earth of what heaven would be like. Each Jew thought of himself for that one day as kingly, and when he read from the Psalms, it was as though he were like the great King David himself.

Of course, they had no movies or television or radio to distract them, and they did not go to football games. They made their Sabbath a day of resting and visiting, prayer, refreshment, study and talk and song. It was a day for strolling, but not too far, a day for the children, a day for friends.

Strict rules for the Sabbath

You sometimes hear stories about how strict the Sabbath rules were in those times, and you hear about pious Jews who even today keep such strict rules. Occasionally these stories are even made to sound a bit funny. We hear of folks who cover up the telephone on Sabbath so the sound of the bell may not break into their Sabbath peace. They will not ride on the Sabbath, because riding means that someone, somewhere, has to work.

In the old days it was a horse that had to work to give people a ride, and the Commandment of the Sabbath was that even the beasts of the field should rest. It is hard for us to understand that this can apply to an automobile, but for the very pious, the rule is the same.

Observant Jews will not carry money on the Sabbath, and this is of course easier to understand. We may think some of their rules, in modern times, have no more meaning, but we understand the idea behind all the rules. The idea is that the troubles and problems of the world shall not enter the Sabbath, not by the tiniest crack. Peace and joy shall not be disturbed.

Cleaning and shopping for the Sabbath

Getting ready for the Sabbath in the old ghetto days was really the busy time of the week. Housewives began to prepare on Thursday, and all day Friday was a very busy time, for everything had to be completely ready a half hour before the sun went down.

First, of course, the house was made spotlessly clean. No matter how poor the family, no matter if the floor was of earth, everything had to be swept and polished and scrubbed to be worthy of the Sabbath bride.

The shopping, begun on Thursday, was hurriedly completed on Friday. One of the main items was the fish for the meal of Sabbath eve—the Friday night meal. If the family was poor, fish might be the only course. If the family was better off, Friday evening was a regular feast, with noodle soup, fish, chicken and all sorts of extra dishes. There was plenty to spare for everyone, and the meal lasted a long, long time.

Each family tried to have a guest. It was a mitzvah to have a guest at the table, especially a stranger in town. So if a stranger was seen in the village,

perhaps a wandering student, everyone tried to get him as a guest for the Friday evening meal. Sometimes the guest was even auctioned off in the synagogue. The man who made the biggest donation got the guest.

A hot meal for the Sabbath day

The big Friday meal was not all that had to be prepared before Sabbath. The housewife had to prepare all the food for the Sabbath day itself. The main dish might be a "cholent," a slow simmering pot of meat and potatoes and vegetables that had a delicious flavor because all the tastes would melt together during the long hours of cooking.

Since it was forbidden to light a fire on Sabbath, the cholent would be started before the sun went down on Friday, and left over a low fire that would last all night and the next day. The cholent would become richer in taste all the time. Many Jews in America, whose parents and grandparents came from the old country, remember the wonderful taste of that Sabbath cholent.

69

There was not only the house to clean and the Sabbath meals to prepare on each busy Friday. All the best clothes had to be cleaned and ironed, and the white tablecloth and the best dishes and silverware were made ready.

Then, too, there was the baking. In those villages, everyone baked her own bread and buns and honeycake and cookies. If a housewife did not do the final baking in her own oven, she prepared the dough and took it to the town baker to place in his big oven.

The Sabbath bread was of course the braided challah. Today you see challah ready-made in the stores. It is sweet tasting and soft, with a light brown crust. But it can never taste like the challah that was made at home in the old days.

Welcoming the Sabbath in the Synagogue

While the women were very busy, the men were also hurrying to finish their work and their business early on Friday, so they could go to the synagogue for the service to welcome the Sabbath. Usually, only the men and boys went for this service. Today in some congregations, the service is held after the Friday meal, and the whole family comes to worship.

The husband would come home from the synagogue after his wife had kindled the Sabbath candles and said her blessing over them. The husband would say "Good Sabbath" to his wife and chil-

Housewives took their challah to the town baker

dren, and bless them. Perhaps he would have been the lucky one at the synagogue to have received the guest in town for his own, and would bring the guest home with him.

Many of our best stories and legends about old-time Jewish life are about Sabbath guests. There are tales of the prophet Elijah, masquerading as a ragged stranger to test whether Jews would take him home as a Sabbath guest. And there are magical tales of wondrous things happening to Jews who had been traveling, and could not quite reach home before sundown for the Sabbath. Perhaps they would have been delayed by a storm or an accident. In some of these stories, a good Jew's horses would suddenly begin to fly, in a cloud, so that he would reach home the moment before the sun went down.

His horse began to fly

The Sabbath evening meal

When father came home, he stood at the Sabbath table and recited the Kiddush over the wine, and then he poured water over his hands for the washing ceremony. After that he recited the blessing over the challah, and broke off a little piece for each person at the table. That first taste of the sweet challah was delicious.

Then the meal would be served. At the meal, if there was a student as a guest or if there was a young boy in the house, there would be Torah talk, and sometimes there would be riddles asked about the Torah.

Everyone liked to show how many quotations he knew by heart. So one person would start with a question, per-

haps a serious question about the soul and whether it comes back to earth in another life. Then the saying of a famous rabbi would be quoted. Then the Talmud might be quoted. Then someone might tell a story about a man who came back to earth as a horse, to work out his debts. The father would ask his son if he thought such a thing was really possible, and perhaps the son would quote the sayings of another famous rabbi. And so a lively conversation would take place.

After the meal, someone would start a song. Then would come one song after another, with everyone joining in.

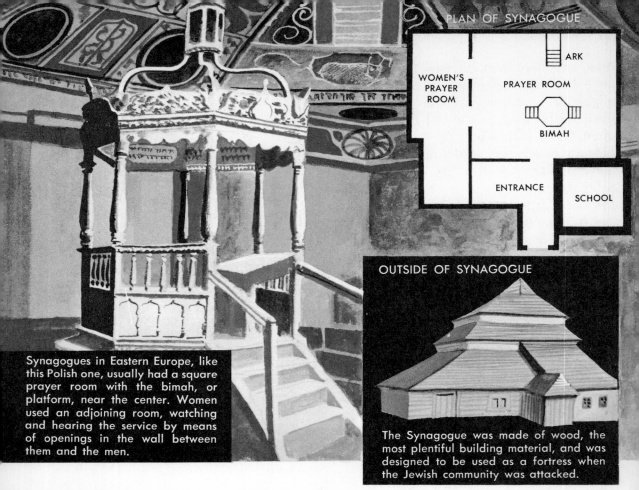

WOMEN'S PRAYER ROOM

PRAYER ROOM

ARK

BIMAH

ENTRANCE

SCHOOL

Synagogues in Eastern Europe, like this Polish one, usually had a square prayer room with the bimah, or platform, near the center. Women used an adjoining room, watching and hearing the service by means of openings in the wall between them and the men.

OUTSIDE OF SYNAGOGUE

The Synagogue was made of wood, the most plentiful building material, and was designed to be used as a fortress when the Jewish community was attacked.

These are special songs called "zmiroth," and you have heard some of them at the Sabbath services, and you can sing them, too.

The younger children would refuse to go to bed, just as they still do. But instead of falling asleep in front of a television set, they would fall asleep at the table, and finally be carried off to bed. The singing would go on for hours.

Sabbath day in the synagogue and at home

Then on Sabbath day, everyone would put on his best clothes. They would stroll around the village, go to the syna-

gogue early, and gossip and visit with each other. In the synagogue, as you know, the men and boys sat together on the main floor, while the women and girls sat in the balcony or behind a special curtain.

Then for the big midday Sabbath meal, the cholent would be served. After the meal, the father usually took a nap. Later on he would spend some time with his sons, asking them test questions to see what they had learned during the week. Then visiting would begin. Relatives and neighbors would come for a little talk and a Sabbath snack of tea and honeycake. Before the afternoon service, there was a regular period of study in the synagogue.

Between the afternoon service and the evening service, the men would drink a little wine or a little schnapps, and there was food and singing and storytelling.

Saying goodbye to the Sabbath

At last when the sun went down there was the Havdalah ceremony, dividing the Sabbath from the rest of the week. Then they said goodbye to the Sabbath bride for another week. Beautiful vessels were used for the wine, and there were special blessings. There was a silver candle holder for the braided candle, and a spice box for sweet smelling spices.

When you look to find the precious things that are handed down in Jewish families from generation to generation, from century to century, it is usually the objects that are part of the Sabbath. The Sabbath candlesticks, the wine goblets, the silver spice boxes. For these were part of that most wonderful day that came once a week, like a day out of heaven.

At the end of that day, people turned to each other and wished each other a good week, the father to the mother, the parents to their friends and to their children—"A good week to you." For ordinary life was lived from Sabbath to Sabbath; and a special life, a life as of kings and queens with no worldly care, was lived on the Sabbath.

THINKING ABOUT WHAT YOU HAVE LEARNED

1. Which Sabbath customs call attention to the basic beliefs of Judaism described in Chapter 3?
2. What made the old-time Sabbath such a day of joy that Jews looked forward to it all week?

QUESTIONS TO ASK YOUR PARENTS

1. Ask your parents (or grandparents) to tell about any happy memories they may have of the Sabbath in their childhood.
2. Do your parents know of any families in the community who still observe the Sabbath as it is described in this chapter?

Havdalah spice box, braided candle, and Kiddush cup

CHAPTER X

A full year of holidays

If every Sabbath brought an air of festivity into the homes of the Jews in the old days, then every holiday was even more a time of wonderful doings. In the older Jewish way of life, every holiday was a great event in the home. The service was in the house of worship, but the celebration was at home.

Passover, the great family holiday

There is one great holiday that still keeps us closest to the old-time ways— Passover. Even for modern Jews, Passover is mainly a family celebration. The biggest part of the observance, the family seder, takes place in the home. There may also be a community seder, with long banquet tables in a large hall. But everyone who can have one at home tries to do so.

In the old days, it was almost as though the Jews became different people during the week of Passover. They wanted to remember that God had freed their forefathers from slavery in Egypt. They wanted to remember the wandering in the wilderness. So they began to bake their matzoh.

The entire house had to be "made pesachdik," or changed for Passover. There would be special dishes, pots, pans, knives, forks, spoons, so that no food eaten during Passover would touch a pot or dish or spoon that was used during the rest of the year. This regulation set Passover apart as a special time.

In many of our homes this rule is still strictly kept. The regular cooking and eating things are packed away, and the Passover things are brought out.

If a family did not own extra sets of pots, then there was a special way of purifying their regular pots and utensils, so they could be used for Passover.

The house was cleaned cleaner than at any time all year, and every speck of non-Passover food was put away, so that on the eve of Passover not a crumb of bread remained in the house. The last job was to search every corner to make sure of this. Many Jews still practice this ceremony.

Special Passover foods

And of course we still have the wonderful Passover foods, from matzoh balls to taiglach, that make the time of Passover such a feast. Today we can buy most of these foods in packages and jars and cans with special kosher-for-Passover labels. There is even Passover ice cream.

In the old days, though, the Jews had never heard of ice cream. And all the Passover dishes were cooked at home. The matzoh balls were patted into shape by the mother's hands, and the children would hang around to poke their fingers in the dough, and then lick it off. Then even Passover wine was made mostly at home. So before Passover the housewife was busy preparing things, as for seven Sabbaths at one time.

But Passover is a family festival in an even larger way than Sabbath. In many families, it has always been the custom for the children to gather for the Passover seder in the home of the grandparents. Some Jewish families do this on Friday nights, too, all through the year. But especially on Passover.

Just before Passover, the married daughters will be busy helping the grandmother to get the feast ready. They may cook some of the dishes in their own homes, and carry the pots to the grandmother's house. In the old days, during the time just before Passover, all the women of the village could be seen shopping for special foods. Daughters and daughters-in-law would exchange recipes and there would be big doings in every kitchen.

Two Seder nights

Most Jews observe two seder nights, as you know, and some people think the

Searching for the Afikomon

reason for this is to give the grand-parents on both sides of the family their chance to have a seder. The real reason is this: The Jewish month begins with the new moon. When the Jews were scattered from Palestine, they were sometimes not exactly sure on which day the new moon appeared. So to be

Lag B'Omer, thirty-three days after Passover

After the big Passover holiday, fifty days went by until the next important holiday. This was Shavuoth, the celebration of giving the Torah to Moses. But fifty days is a long time to go without a holiday, so in between, on the thirty-third day after Passover, there came a very jolly event, Lag B'Omer. On Lag B'Omer young people would go out to picnic in the woods, and sometimes they would hold archery contests.

This Lag B'Omer custom is in memory of Rabbi Akiba and his students. For

safe, they had the seder on two nights instead of one. But as it has turned out to be so convenient for the two sets of grandparents, the custom has remained, even now that we can be sure of the calendar.

In the old days, before Passover the grandfather would open his Shulchan Aruch, and study it to make sure that every regulation was followed.

as you know, Rabbi Akiba lived during the time of Roman rule in Palestine. Because the Romans forbade Jews to study the Torah, Rabbi Akiba and his pupils had to do this in secret. They would go out in the woods, and pretend to be hunting. And while the scouts were posted like hunters with bows and arrows, the rest of the group would gather and discuss the Torah.

Celebrating the giving of the Torah on Shavuoth

Lag B'Omer is a spring holiday; but with the beginning of summer comes Shavuoth, the festival of the first fruits. To celebrate the giving of the Torah, in the old days in Europe, green plants were brought into each house, and into each schoolroom. The home and the "cheder" blossomed with life, as the knowledge of the Torah is life.

There was feasting for Shavuoth, too. Blintzes and kreplach were the special dishes. Plates were piled high with these treats and all the students, especially those who were poor, would go from house to house eating blintzes and kreplach.

The fast of Tisha B'Ab

In the midst of summer comes another religious observance, Tisha B'Ab. This is not a feast. It is a fast. It comes on the 9th day of the month of Ab. This is the terrible date in the Jewish calendar that marked the fall of the Temple in Jerusalem, not only once, but twice. For both the First Temple and the Second Temple were destroyed on that same terrible date, though hundreds of years apart. The first time, as you remember, was when the Jews were taken as captives to Babylon, and the second time was when the Romans conquered Palestine.

On the 9th of Ab, every household in the old Jewish villages became still. The people passed the day in the synagogue saying prayers and reading the Book of Lamentations. And many wept for this sad day.

Rosh Hashanah begins the fall holidays

Then, at the end of summer, comes the Jewish New Year. This begins a time called the Ten Days of Penitence which lasts through Yom Kippur. It is a time for us to think about what is good and what is bad, and how we have behaved all year. We mostly observe Rosh Hashanah in the synagogue, but it is also

A Sukkah decorated for the holiday

an important holiday in the home. It is the beginning of ten days called the High Holiday Season.

To start off the High Holidays, families used to buy new clothes and new shoes, and everyone would come to the synagogue in these new things. And in the evening at home, there would be a feast which would start with something especially sweet. Just as at Passover we eat bitter things to remind us of Jewish suffering in the past, so at Rosh Hashanah we eat sweet things to remind us that the future can be good. Usually the Rosh Hashanah sweet was an apple dipped in honey.

Yom Kippur, a day of fasting

The High Holiday week ends with Yom Kippur. Yom Kippur again is a solemn fast day, for it is the time to ask forgiveness for our sins. During the day of fasting, pious Jews prayed in the synagogue. On the day before, they had visited each other at home, to ask

forgiveness for any wrongs they might have done during the year.

People who had not been speaking to each other for months would fall into each other's arms, and say how foolish it is to have quarrels in our short lives on earth. And they gave charity, for in this way man cared for his fellow men. Many enemies had become friends again, and the year was starting out with no anger amongst good Jews.

Eating outdoors on Sukkoth

As soon as Yom Kippur was over, in the old-time Jewish villages, each family got busy preparing for the next festival, Sukkoth. This is a holiday like our Thanksgiving. In fact, our Pilgrim fathers thought of Thanksgiving when they read about Sukkoth in the Bible.

Jews built little huts for outdoor eating during Sukkoth. The hut was called a Sukkah. Sometimes these huts stood from year to year; only the roof needed to be covered with new branches and leaves, each time Sukkoth came around. And during the whole of Sukkoth, all the family meals were eaten in them.

Hanukah comes in winter

Then as winter came, there was Hanukah, the festival of lights and of religious freedom. We still keep much of the spirit of Hanukah in our homes in modern times, with the lighting of candles and with special gifts, and with special games like the dreidl. And some of us also keep the old-time custom of the latke party, when everyone eats potato pancakes.

Purim, the gayest holiday

At the end of winter, comes Purim. In the Jewish villages, this was again a time for gifts from one household to another. Even the poorest would make some little cakes and delicacies, and bring them to their neighbors and friends. Housewives would try to outdo each other with their cookery and storekeepers would send gifts to all their customers.

But Purim was also a public festival. In the synagogue, they read the story of Mordecai and Esther from the Megillah and the story of Purim would be acted out before all the Jews in the village. Nowadays, in Israel, Purim is the great spring festival, with children's pageants and parades in the streets, with masquerade parties and balls. We have large Purim parties in our synagogues and temples and centers, and we have Purim parties in our homes, too. Purim is the gayest of all the Jewish holidays.

Soon after Purim, it was time to prepare for Passover. And in the old towns, the housewives would begin to turn their homes inside out in the big job of cleaning, for the great yearly cycle of holidays was ending and beginning again.

Holidays linked the Jewish way of life

So from Sabbath to Sabbath, from holiday to holiday, the Jewish way of life was linked together. It was linked not only through worship in the synagogue, but through feasts and family gatherings. As each holiday ended, it was time to talk about the next one, and to get things ready for it. There were special dishes to cook, new clothes to sew and to buy for Rosh Hashanah. There was the Sukkoth hut to build. There were masquerade costumes to make for Purim.

THINKING ABOUT WHAT YOU HAVE LEARNED

1. Which is your favorite holiday? Why? Which might be the favorite of a Jewish boy in Hungary a century ago?
2. In comparing the observance of these holidays with our own observances today, which have changed the most? Which the least?

QUESTIONS TO ASK YOUR PARENTS

1. How does the fasting on Yom Kippur truly make a difference for many Jews and help them to observe it is a day of atonement?
2. Which Jewish holiday foods are favorites in your home?

CHAPTER XI

The events of a lifetime

How does your life unfold itself from the time you were a baby? First you noticed your mother, then there was your family around you in your home, then as you grew you noticed the community in which you live. And in the same way, like a circle inside a bigger circle inside a bigger circle, are the events of your life.

Life cycle begins at birth

There are certain great events in each life. The first of course is to be born. That is when the cycle of life begins. And every people in the world, from the savages to the most civilized, has a way of celebrating the birth of a baby.

Aside from the religious celebration, nowadays we send gifts and cards for the baby and the mother. In the old-time Jewish customs, there were no special cards, but there was a special ribbon to tie around the baby's crib, inscribed for good luck with quotations from the Bible or from the prayer book. Many visitors would come to the house, bringing gifts.

But the birth of a baby was also a time for religious expression. Students of the Torah would come to sit by the bedside and say prayers for the new-born baby.

If the baby was a boy, there was a great event on the eighth day. This was called the "brith." Today we still have the custom of the brith. Today this custom may be carried out in the hospital before the baby is brought home. But in old times after the circumcision the family usually gave a big party with good things to eat and drink. If the baby was a girl, the father came to the synagogue to have her named and blessed.

Redemption of the first-born

If the baby boy was the first-born, when he was one month old, there was another custom to follow. On that day, the parents gave a gift as a reminder of the days of the Temple in Jerusalem, when parents brought such a gift to the priests. It was called a redemption, which means reclaiming by giving something else in exchange.

And what was reclaimed? The child himself. For the old idea was that each first-born male child belonged to the service of the priests of the Temple. But the parents could redeem the child with a gift. This gift was called "Pidyon Ha-Ben."

A boy's first day in school

Then there was another big day reserved for boys. In those times, as you know, few girls were permitted to go to school. The boy's first day in school was a day of celebration. It was a custom to put honey on the pages of his book, so that the boy should start to school feeling that learning was going to be something sweet in his life.

The thirteenth birthday

The next important event in the life cycle was the thirteenth birthday. This too was reserved for boys. It was the Bar Mitzvah, which meant that the boy was old enough and knew enough to take his place in the community and to pray in the congregation. Indeed, Bar Mitzvah boys were considered as men, old enough to become engaged, get married, and go to work.

Of course, a boy did not usually get married and start a household at thirteen. But he might become engaged, and go to live with his future in-laws, who would support him while he continued his studies.

The first day of school

The ceremony of the Bar Mitzvah took place, as it does today, in the synagogue. The boy was called up to recite the blessings over the Torah, to read his portion and to make a little speech showing his learning. Today, many of our congregations also have a similar ceremony for girls, the Bat Mitzvah.

We have kept a very important part of the Bar Mitzvah, which takes place after the synagogue service, and that is the celebration at home. Sometimes, in fact, these celebrations become such big family events that they are held in hotels.

The gifts are not quite like the presents one gets for an ordinary birthday. The Bar Mitzvah boy in the old days, and today, received coming-of-age gifts, such as a Bible, a new prayer book, perhaps a tallis, and even a fountain pen.

Nowadays we do not consider that a boy of thirteen is ready to go to work. And if we study the old-time Jewish life we find that the burdens of a grown man were not often put on a boy of thirteen. More often he would be apprenticed to learn a trade, or if his parents were in business he would begin to learn the business.

Girls educated at home

The girls meanwhile were prepared for the most important event of their lives, marriage. They learned to cook, to keep house and to take care of young children. Often, too, they were taught to read and write at home, and they were taught sewing and embroidering. But they did not go to school to study the

Torah. Women were given only a home education.

Marriages arranged by a "shadchen"

And there was not the same kind of courtship that we know today. Boys and girls did not have dates and go to dances. If they lived in the same village, of course they saw each other as they grew up. A boy and girl who liked each other could somehow let their parents know that they hoped one day to "make a match." But often the matches were made without even asking the opinion of the groom or bride.

There were special matchmakers. Such a person was known as a "shadchen." He would keep a list of the boys and girls in his own town. And he would travel and write letters to keep in touch with other matchmakers, so as to know about marriage prospects far and wide.

A rich Jew would want a gifted scholar for his daughter, and word would go out among the matchmakers to be on the lookout for a very bright boy. Sometimes these boys were poor but this did not matter so much. It was an honor to secure a son-in-law who was a genius in the Torah.

A Jewish wedding in medieval Germany

Bride's family offered a dowry

The bride's family had to offer a dowry to the young man. A dowry would help a young couple get started in life. And if the boy was to continue his studies, they might live on the dowry for years.

If a family was too poor to provide a dowry for the daughter, there was a community dowry fund, so that poor girls would be able to get married. For no matter how pretty a girl was, in those days it was very hard to get married with no dowry at all.

Today we don't have the same system, but we often have the same idea. Parents will give large wedding gifts in order to help a young couple get started in life. But today the boy's parents will help out just as much as the girl's parents, simply depending on which can afford to provide the most help. And of course there are many couples who want to start out on their own without any special help.

The marriage ceremony

Next to birth, the great event in the life cycle was marriage.

The wedding took place under a "chuppah" or canopy that was held up on four poles. This custom is still used in many Jewish weddings. In the traditional ceremony, the groom stood under the canopy, and the bride was

83

led around him several times. In the very old tradition, the rabbi read the benedictions and then the bride and groom drank from a wine glass, and the groom stepped on the glass and broke it.

One explanation of the breaking of the glass is that it reminds people of the destruction of the Temple in Jerusalem. So even in their happiest moment Jews do not forget Jerusalem.

In the old days every wedding was a great event for the whole community. It was a special honor to invite the poor. There are tales of big weddings where the bride's father would send wagons to distant towns to bring all the poor that could be found, for the marriage feast.

An important part of the wedding was the reading of the "Ketubah," or marriage contract. In the old way of life this was an important document. It told exactly what the families promised to the bride and groom. These documents were beautifully decorated by scribes, with colorful designs of birds and flowers. You can see samples of

Ketuboth in museums of history and art.

After the ceremony there was music, usually by fiddlers, and there was dancing long into the night.

Ceremonies for death

The married couple would continue the life cycle when their own children were born and grew up and were married. The end of the great cycle naturally comes when a person dies. Then, there are ceremonies to be observed, too.

In the traditional Jewish way, the family remains in the house for seven days, sitting on low stools. This is called "sitting shiveh." In the old Jewish way of life, the members of the family would not leave the house except to go to the synagogue on the Sabbath. The men did not go to work, and the women did no housework. Their friends would come and take care of the house, and would bring them their meals or cook for them in their own home. During the seven days, the family thought and talked about the

A Jewish funeral in Italy

person who had died, and many visitors came, friends and relatives, to talk with them.

The men of the family recited the special prayer of kaddish every day for eleven months, and after that on every anniversary of the death. Thus, the memory of the person remained a part of the family.

When a first son was born, there was always great rejoicing in a family, for this meant there was a son who would grow up and be ready to say kaddish to remember the older people when they died. This idea was so important that a son was even called "a kaddish." Through the son, the family knew that the cycle of Jewish life would keep on.

THINKING ABOUT WHAT YOU HAVE LEARNED

1. Ceremonial events in the life of a Jew are usually referred to with Hebrew names. Can you tell the meaning of each of the following: Bar Mitzvah, Ketubah, Kaddish, Brith, Pidyon Ha-Ben, Chuppah, Shadchen, Shiveh, Tallis.
2. There is a Hebrew prayer that is recited at many of the happy events described in this chapter. It is called the she-he-che-yo-nu. It thanks God for keeping us alive until this time. At which of the ceremonies we have just read about do you think it is recited?

QUESTIONS TO ASK YOUR PARENTS

1. Why do Jews feel that all of life's important events should be observed by religious ceremonials?
2. Ask your parents how they would compare our customs of marriage with the old customs of a matchmaker and a dowry.

CHAPTER XII

A woman's way

We have learned so much about the importance of sons, that it would be easy to believe that girls were not very important in the old-time Jewish way of life. But this would be a wrong idea.

It is true that the main actions of life seemed to be centered around men and their doings. It was the men only who studied the Torah, and it was the men who recited the group prayers to God, and a man was needed to recite kaddish. It was the men who decided what was right and what was wrong. So it would seem as if the old world was certainly a man's world, as if the men had all the rights, and the women were only the property of the men.

But things are not always what they seem. And things can change. Today we know that women have the same opportunities as men. They go to schools and colleges with men, and have careers like men if they wish. They can be teachers and doctors and managers and lawyers.

Your teacher in religious school, as well as in your public school, may be a woman. But in old times, this would have been strange. Women were not likely to be teachers, because they may not even have gone to school themselves. Even after women began to teach in the regular schools, the teachers in the Jewish schools were men.

Women were respected

Yet while we know that women couldn't do as many things as women do today, we must not conclude that women were less important in the family. From our oldest Bible stories, you can see how women were respected, and what an important part they had in all the family decisions. We know the wives of the patriarchs as well as we know the patriarchs: Sarah and Rebecca and Leah and Rachel are as close to us as Abraham, Isaac and Jacob.

Abraham consulted his wife Sarah whenever an important family question arose. And Moses sought the advice of his sister Miriam. And it was a woman, the prophetess Deborah, who first urged the men of Israel to unite to defeat their enemies.

A special education for girls

It is not only from stories of Biblical times, but from books and tales about Jewish life in Europe, that we can understand the important place of the woman in the household. The raising of a daughter who could carry on the ways of her people meant a very complicated education of a special kind— the girl's kind.

In the Bible, we read how Abraham sent his most trusted servant far across the land, to find a bride for his son Isaac. For Abraham wanted a bride from among his own people, who were still in the faraway land that he had left when he set out to seek the land God had promised to him. Abraham wanted his son to marry a girl who had been taught to know the ways of life that belonged to his own people.

The first and most important thing that a girl learned was to continue the customs that kept the family and the tribe together. The men worried about the laws, but the women kept the customs.

Rules for keeping a kosher kitchen

And it was through the home education that every girl learned to give Jewish life its special quality, its own flavor. In the Jewish life in Europe, the girls learned to prepare the special dishes, such as gefilte fish and cholent for the Sabbath. They also learned the very

Deborah encourages the soldiers

complicated rules of keeping a kosher kitchen. For hundreds of years those rules were strictly kept in all Jewish homes.

A girl learned to keep separate sets of dishes for milk foods and for meat foods. She learned how to tell meat that could be eaten from meat that could not be eaten according to the tradition.

If you think it was simple to learn such things, remember that there are whole books printed about Jewish holiday dishes alone. The Jewish girl learned how to bring Sabbath into the home, and how to purify the house for Passover.

Household tasks had religious importance

As you see, the household tasks were not merely household tasks. They had

a religious importance. The rabbis said the home was a "Small Temple" and the woman its priestess. And that is what gave the woman added importance in the family. She had to make sure that everything in the house was done exactly according to the Jewish regulations.

Women took part in family business

We know also that women in the old world towns often took the main part in the family business. If the husband was a scholar, he might sit and study the Talmud all day long, while his wife tended to worldly affairs. She might take care of a store, or of a stand in the

Jewish women in a Polish marketplace

marketplace. If the family owned property, it would be the woman who dealt with the tenants.

In Yiddish stories about life in Russia or Poland, we often read of such women who made it possible for their husbands to spend their time in studying the holy books.

Bringing up children

Rearing the children was also her trust, and this was more of a task than it is today, especially in the case of girls. For while the boys would go to the Talmud Torah, the girls learned everything at home. To raise a girl and teach her the many things that she now learns at school was not easy. In the old world, mothers had to teach their daughters cooking and sewing and housekeeping; and they often taught them to read and write.

Stories in Yiddish for women

In fact, while the men studied in Hebrew, the women used the Yiddish language. Because of this, the first popular stories of Jewish life were written for women. Just as today some of our best magazines are known as women's magazines, the lively stories of the old days were written for feminine readers.

When we think about it, the life of women has changed less than it would seem. Women are now free to have all kinds of careers and to have the same education as men. But they still prefer, quite naturally, to devote themselves to keeping the home and raising the family. It is through them that the customs and ideals of the whole people are carried on.

Women in the synagogue

In the synagogue, in the old days, the women sat in their own section. They did not count in a minyan, for the

prayer group had to be made up of at least ten *men*. There was a special book of prayers for women, with a Yiddish translation and stories. Often there would be only a few women in the synagogue who knew how to read. These few would read the prayers and the rest of the women would repeat the words after them.

Women and men in partnership

In the beginning, when human beings lived by hunting, it was the men, who were bigger and stronger, who seemed more important. So the men made the rules and gave the orders for each group. But as civilization grew, we came to see life as a partnership between men and women. And Jewish ways have changed to keep up with these growing ideas.

But it is good to see that even in our oldest days, in Biblical times, the woman was honored and respected and sought after and loved. In fact, the oldest love stories of mankind are the stories in our Bible, like the story of Jacob and Rachel, and the story of Boaz and Ruth.

THINKING ABOUT WHAT YOU HAVE LEARNED

1. In what ways did the Jewish women of the ghetto help to keep Judaism alive in the home?
2. Some congregations have introduced the Bat Mitzvah ceremony for girls. What would the Jews of the ghetto have thought of this idea?

QUESTIONS TO ASK YOUR PARENTS

1. Which women in the Bible are your mother's favorites to show the importance of women in Judaism?
2. What have been the greatest changes in the position of the Jewish women today as compared to the time described in this chapter?

Blessing the Sabbath candles

CHAPTER XIII

Charity, kindness and good deeds

Some day you may hear the words, "The Jews take care of their own." That means the Jews take care of all Jews who are in need. They help the sick, the old and the unfortunate.

Many kinds of charities

That does not mean that Jews help only Jews. And it does not mean that Jews are the only people who are charitable. If you look at the letters that come to your home, asking for contributions for hospitals, or for old-age homes, you will see that they are not all for Jewish groups. People help people, whether or not they belong to the same religion.

Besides the charities that are given in the name of religious groups, there are general groups, called non-sectarian. And there are social service organizations and relief organizations and health organizations. There are free camps for children and charity homes of many kinds. Yet, there is truth to the saying that "Jews take care of their own."

For it is natural that people help first those in their own family who need help, or those in their own group. And in the case of the Jews, in the old days there was no other way for a Jew to be helped. In many countries the Jews did not receive any share of public help, even though they paid a large share of the taxes. They had to support their own schools, sick-houses, old-age homes and other charities.

A promise to Peter Stuyvesant

When the very first Jews came to America, a small group landed in New Amsterdam, which is now New York. And the governor of New Amsterdam, Peter Stuyvesant, finally gave them permission to settle there. But the first condition he made was that they had to guarantee that none of the Jewish people would ask for public help. The Jews had to take care of their own.

It was easy for the Jews to agree to this, since they had done so wherever they lived. It was part of their way of life. They had always given help to non-Jewish charities as well. Today, as Jews help non-Jews, many non-Jews

help Jewish causes. When Jewish charities are raising money, there are always non-Jews who make donations.

"Tzedakah" is a great mitzvah

To the Jew, it was always a holy act to help the needy. It was a great mitzvah. Next to studying the Torah, it was said, the greatest mitzvah is charity. Indeed, one of the rabbis quoted in the Talmud, Rav Assi, said, "Charity is equal to all mitzvoth."

The word for charity, "tzedakah," comes from the Hebrew word, "tzedek," which means "righteousness." You have heard the word for a saintly wise man, a "tzadik." That word comes from the same root. What is right is holy, and charity is a holy, right thing to do. So charity is tzedakah.

Thus tzedakah is woven into the cycle of Jewish life. Every event in that cycle, in the old world, was made a time for tzedakah. The birth of a baby was a time to make a donation to the poor. A Bar Mitzvah, a wedding, a funeral— all these were times when Jews put money in the tzedakah boxes, or gave the rabbi money to distribute to the needy.

Every holiday was a time to make gifts, so that no Jew would be left without the means of observing the holiday.

Tzedakah boxes

There were special little collection boxes, or tzedakah boxes, that were kept in every house. We still see such boxes today. For instance, the Keren Kayemeth, the Jewish National Fund, collects money in this way to buy land in Israel. These are the little blue-and-white boxes which you see in grocery shops and in candy stores and in offices; people also have these boxes at home. Many Jews make it a habit to drop all their pennies and nickels into these boxes. From the money collected in these little Keren Kayemeth boxes, land was bought in Palestine, to belong to the whole Jewish people.

You may see other such boxes with the names of different charities on them. There are collection boxes for old age homes, and for colleges of Jewish studies. But in modern times we also have big campaigns to collect large sums of money for public needs. A number of Jewish social service groups will get together to hold such a campaign, and then they will share the funds that are collected, so that every charity is taken care of.

Best to give in secret

In the old days, people lived in smaller groups where everybody knew everybody, and their charity system was simpler. Donations were made through a rabbi or through a leader in the community. Often these gifts were anonymous. The Jews considered that the best way to give charity was in secret. This thought went all the way back to the days of the Temple in Jerusalem. In the Temple, it was said, there was a room where people could leave money without being seen. Anyone who needed money could come and get it without being asked any questions.

But there are also people who feel proud that they can give money to the community. In our big campaigns today, you will see that both kinds of givers are among us. When a large meeting is held to raise money for the United Jewish Appeal, or perhaps for building a new center, or for any other cause, sometimes the gifts will be announced by a speaker. He will announce the name of each donor, and the amount, and everyone at the meeting will applaud his friends for their generosity.

A tzedakah box

Still there will always be some donors who have their gifts announced without their names. The announcer will say, "Anonymous." These people believe in the ancient idea that giving should be done in secret.

The Talmud tells how to give

All through the ages, Jews have studied the question of tzedakah, not only of giving, but of how to give. And the Talmud tells us many things about this subject. It tells us, "Better is he who gives little to charity from money honestly earned, than he who gives much from dishonestly gained wealth." It tells us, "Let a man beware of giving carelessly, without inquiry into the worth of the applicant."

It tells us, "Charity knows neither race nor creed." And this saying explains the rule in the Bible that not only Jews but gentiles shall be allowed to gather grain left on the field by the reapers. We all remember this from the story of Ruth.

Maimonides' "Ladder of Tzedakah"

The Jewish ideas about charity, from the Bible, the Talmud, and from all the rabbinical books of wisdom, were put into a simple code by the great scholar, Maimonides. It is called the "Ladder of Tzedakah." And it tells us the eight degrees of charity, in order of increasing importance:

94

1. *Giving unwillingly.*

   Lowest on the ladder is the man who gives only because he is forced to do so. This is a gift of the hand but not of the heart.

2. *Giving less than one should, but cheerfully.*

   Of course one should not give less than one should. Even so, if the gift is made with good will, its smallness is partly redeemed.

3. *Giving after being asked.*

   It is almost as good as giving before being asked, if one gives cheerfully, and as much as one can.

4. *Giving before being asked.*

   When we see a need, it is good to give without waiting to be asked. But we may spoil our giving if we make too much of a show of it, and embarrass the one who receives.

5. *Giving without knowing the receiver.*

   The needy person may know from whom the gift has come. But the giver does not know to whom it went.

6. *Giving anonymously to someone you know is needy.*

   This is what happens when an anonymous gift is made, but to a person who is known to be needy.

7. *Giving anonymously to an anonymous person.*

   This is the best way to give.

8. *Helping a person to help himself.*

   To help a person to find work, or to learn a trade, to give a person a loan to start in business, is the highest form of charity.

Giving is godly

From this list, we see how much thought the Jews have always given to charity. Indeed, there is a saying in the Bible, "He who is gracious to the poor lends to the Lord." (Prov. 19:17) And, in the Talmud "By the side of the poor stands God himself, pleading for His stricken children." And again, "He that feeds the hungry feeds himself too, for charity blesses him that gives even more than him that takes." To give to the needy has always been considered to be godly.

But no man could feel himself to be a god, because his own good fortune came from God. He was only returning a part of it to the poor. The Jews knew too well from their bad times that any one of them, even the largest giver, might one day need help.

Special organizations for tzedakah

As Jewish communities grew, life became more complicated. In a small Jewish town in the old country, everyone could know who was in need. In such a village, you could pass a man's house and see at once whether he had wood for his fire. But in large modern commu-

Visiting the sick

nities, charity has to be done with a system.

Even in the old-time Jewish towns, there came to be special organizations for each charity task. You hear people speaking of "my favorite charity," which means there is one kind of need that touches them most deeply. So in an old-time Jewish town, people found their favorite charities. One woman might take it on herself to collect clothing for the needy. Another might feel that the most important thing she could do would be to collect dowries for poor girls, so they could get married.

Through such persons, there grew to be special charities, with special funds for each need. There were charities for orphan homes, for hospitals, for schools for the poor. And there were special funds for taking care of needy strangers.

There were groups of people who collected money to make loans without interest. Such a loan might help a family through an emergency, such as an operation. Or it might help a Jew to help himself by starting a small business. In this country today, we still have Jewish groups making loans of this kind. And in the old towns there were funds for Passover supplies for the poor, and funds for burial expenses, and such funds still exist in many Jewish communities throughout the world.

Gifts of good-heartedness

The people who have the most generous hearts are not always the ones who have the most money to give away. Indeed, the Talmud warns us, "Let a man be generous in his charities, but let him beware of giving away all that he has."

But people with little money can add another kind of gift, the gift of kindness, and of their time and effort. Such gifts are known as "g'miluth chassadim." They are the gifts of good-heartedness, such as visiting the sick or comforting people who have a death in the family. The "gray ladies" in our hospitals of today, who regularly give their time to cheering up invalids, are performing a charity of this kind.

The Talmud tells us that g'miluth chassadim, or benevolence, is superior to mere almsgiving in three ways: Almsgiving is performed with money, and benevolence with the heart. Almsgiving is limited to the poor, but kindness is a gift to the rich as well as the poor. Almsgiving is only for the living, but sympathy is for the dead as well as the living.

In the old style village community, it was as though every Jew were part of a great family, and charity and benevolence could go hand in hand. The charity of Jews went far beyond their own circle, even in the days of the ghetto. Today it is quite easy for us to know the needs of Jews and of other people all over the world.

Still, it is only natural that Jews keep first in mind the needs of other Jews, and that is why we say that charity, or tzedakah, begins at home.

THINKING ABOUT WHAT YOU HAVE LEARNED

1. Suppose you have some money to give away. How does the Jewish idea of tzedakah help you to decide to whom the money should be given?
2. Why did Maimonides think it is a higher type of charity when the giver does not know to whom he gives?

QUESTIONS TO ASK YOUR PARENTS

1. What are some of the Jewish and non-Jewish tzedakah funds in your community?
2. Is giving to a temple called tzedakah too?

CHAPTER XIV

The Way of the plain folk

Not all Jews in the old days spent their time in studying the holy books. In the villages, Jews worked at all kinds of jobs. Many were simple wagon drivers or even water carriers, for in most towns the water had to be brought from the village well or from a stream.

Water carriers and wood choppers and bread bakers and shoemakers, and tailors did not have much time to study the Talmud. A plain Jew might refer to the Shulchan Aruch for his rules and regulations; but the man who was really respected could quote from memory examples and explanations from the Talmud and all the other books of the law.

A secret knowledge

The plain people felt in their hearts that there was something in their religion besides the rules and regulations of the Talmud and the Shulchan Aruch. They longed for the true feeling of understanding God. Some believed that this feeling could be satisfied only through studies. They believed that there was a secret, mysterious knowledge that could be found buried in the holy books.

There were many pious men who believed this message was written in a kind of code. And many simple Jews, the bakers and the shoemakers, waited for their pious scholars to discover the code, the secret message that would tell them the day when the Messiah would come! They dreamed that the Messiah would lead them back to the Holy Land, and a life of peace.

When the Messiah comes

In far-off Poland and in Russia there sometimes were pogroms. Ignorant people who hated the Jews would rob, beat and even kill Jews. Then the Jews would pray for the Messiah. They would ask each other, and ask their rabbis, "Where will the Messiah first appear? When?" They thought and dreamed of Messiah as a real person, and one of their favorite songs was about "when Messiah comes," and how wonderful everything would be from that day on!

Everyone would eat raisins and nuts and all sorts of good things "when the Messiah comes."

When all the sensible explanations failed to give them the answer to the question of their dreams, they tried to find magical explanations. And so they turned to the "cabalists" who made magical explanations out of the letters of words in the Bible.

Magic in Hebrew letters

A cabalist would take the first letter of each word in a Biblical verse, and put these letters together to make new words. Or else cabalists tried numerology. You know that in Hebrew writing, the letters of the Hebrew alphabet stand for numbers. You can change a word into numbers, or you can add up the numbers in a word, or do all sorts of numerical tricks with it.

Suppose it was the year 5412 and a cabalist would be trying to find the answer to "when will the Messiah come?" He would find some words of prophecy in the Bible. And he would add up the letters in those words, and the total might be 5413. Then he would announce, "Jews! Take heart! The Messiah is coming next year! I can prove it!"

False Messiahs

In bad times, when Jews were driven out of Spain and out of England, when they fled from one country to another, they were ready to believe any word of hope. The magical scholars would fast and pray and draw circles on the ground and speak magic charms, and then they would make their predictions.

The cabalists would wander from town to town. Sometimes a cabalist even came to believe that he himself was the Messiah. And he might tell

A cabalist drawing magic circles

people to give up their homes, and follow him to Palestine. Such men were Sabbatai Zvi and Solomon Molcho. But each time such a leader arose, it turned out to be a false dream. For his followers were usually robbed and beaten and even killed on their way to the Holy Land.

But because so many Jews were ready to believe each false Messiah, we realize how strongly the Jews longed for the day when they could be free in their own country. When you want something very badly, you are ready to believe almost any story that promises it to you. For instance, suppose you want very badly to take a trip to Israel. And suppose someone came running into your house and said, "Listen! Our whole class has been awarded a trip to Israel!" You would listen and believe at first, because the trip is just what you want.

But after you had been disappointed a few times, you would need some other kind of proof.

And that was what happened with the Jewish people a few hundred years ago. Many times they had been disappointed. And so they wanted a new hope of happiness.

The Baal Shem Tov

This came to them from a great man whose name was Israel, and who was called the "Baal Shem Tov," which means "master of the good Name." As you remember, the name of God is not known. When God spoke to Moses he said, "I am what I am; I will be what I will be." But through the centuries

The Hassidim believe in the joy of life

there have been legends that the unknown Name can become known to a few extremely pious Jews.

And we have such legends about Rabbi Israel, a real person, who lived in a small town in the Carpathian mountains.

He was said to be an orphan who grew up and became the caretaker of a little synagogue. He is said to have known not only the whole Talmud, but the secret and mysterious Cabala. But Rabbi Israel did not try to make magical predictions or to show off his great learning. Instead, he made the way to God very simple.

Truest worship straight from the heart

He said a Jew did not have to be an expert in the Torah, to worship God better, for he said the truest worship was straight from the heart.

One day when an ignorant shepherd boy wandered into the synagogue and began to whistle in happiness, Rabbi Israel was delighted. He said that a boy who did not know his prayers, but who whistled because he was happy and loved God and loved God's world, was sending up to heaven the most beautiful prayers of all.

Rabbi Israel told the Jews they could worship God through laughter and through singing and through dancing, as well as through repeating the regular prayers. He told them that doing good to people was more important than knowing all the rules of the Shulchan Aruch.

He told them that the spirit of the law was important, and that to observe the letter of the law without the spirit was not good. Today, some Jews feel that the spiritual teachings of the Baal Shem Tov express our modern need for faith in God.

The spirit of the Bible is reawakened

He taught God's word to the common people, the wagon drivers and the water carriers, by telling them stories with a moral. You can read some of these stories in library books today.

And his words were like a fresh, fragrant wind to the plain Jew. For many Jews had come to pay so much attention to the law that they lost much of the spirit of Jewish life. If we go back to the beginning we find that spirit and that beauty in the Bible itself. The Bible is filled with wonderful tales, to teach us what is right and what is wrong. The Bible has songs about the beauty of life, such as the Psalms of King David and the Song of Songs of King Solomon. It was this spirit that Rabbi Israel, the Baal Shem Tov, reawakened.

And thus, more and more people came to Rabbi Israel. Soon they began to tell stories of his wisdom, and tales of miracles he had done.

His followers would describe the long nights that he spent in prayer, and they would tell of terrible disasters that had been prevented by his prayers. They would tell how Jew-haters were stopped from killing innocent Jews, or how murderers who tried to throw blame on a Jew for their own crimes were found out, because of the vision of the Baal Shem Tov. They would tell legends of how bandits in the woods became petrified and could not move their arms or their legs, when the Baal Shem Tov drove by in his wagon.

Hassidim and tzadikim

On the Sabbath, many students would gather to join in the Sabbath joy of the Baal Shem Tov. They danced and sang, and the plain people would come and be welcomed. The plain people loved this new understanding of the Jewish religion. More and more they followed the joyous way of the Baal Shem Tov. and they became known as "hassidim" or "the righteous ones."

Some of the Baal Shem Tov's students became leaders or "rebbes," and spread his ideas to different towns. A rebbe who was especially wise and pure was called a "tzadik," and a number of the Baal Shem Tov's followers became tzadikim.

After the Baal Shem died, these tzadikim were worshipped almost like kings. A Jew would travel far to consult a tzadik. He would ask advice on whether to buy or sell a business, whether to marry or divorce. He would bring valuable gifts to the rebbe.

Misnagdim opposed to Hassidism

Not all Jews followed the Hassidic rebbes. Those who believed strongly in the older ways of worship and study made fun of the Hassidim. They called

The bandits became petrified

the Hassidim ignorant and superstitious. But there were Hassidim who were very learned. And the Hassidim were also quite strict about the rules of Jewish life for Sabbath and the holidays and for kosher food. The great difference was that they wanted more spirit in their worship. They danced and they sang in the synagogue. In this way they felt that the common man could come just as close to God as the learned talmudist.

Those who were against the Hassidim believed that religion should be more dignified. They did not want to believe in miracles and in wonder-workers. So the Jewish population became divided between the Hassidim and the Misnagdim, which means the opposition or the "againsters." Some of the "againsters" even declared that the Hassidim could not be thought of as Jews!

As time went on, there came Hassidic leaders who were not as wise and not as pure as the Baal Shem Tov. There were Hassidic rabbis who demanded large gifts for their favors, and who became rich and powerful. This gave the other side good reason to attack them.

A simple and joyful faith

But the pure idea of Hassidism was an idea that helped to bring back many Jews to the simple and great faith of their religion. Though there were many jokes about the Hassidim, told by the opposition, there were also many stories of their good deeds.

When the Jewish communities of Europe were destroyed by the Nazis, numbers of Hassidim found their way to Israel and to America. They still carry on their own way of worship and their own customs.

Today, some of our greatest scholars have studied the ideas of the Hassidim, and written books about them. Martin Buber, a professor at the Hebrew University in Jerusalem, has written books about the Baal Shem Tov and other Hassidic rebbes, showing how deep and how beautiful and how important their ideas were.

These books, and other books of charming Hassidic stories, help us to taste the flavor of life in the old country and to see where some of the ideas in our own way of life come from. For it was as though Hassidism made Jewish life young and joyful all over again.

THINKING ABOUT WHAT YOU HAVE LEARNED

1. Why was the Baal Shem Tov able to win such a large number of followers?
2. Why were some Jews opposed to Hassidism?

QUESTIONS TO ASK YOUR PARENTS

1. How do the Jews of your congregation feel about the coming of a Messiah?
2. The Hassidim believe that singing, dancing and laughter should be a part of worship. How do the Jews of your congregation feel about this?

CHAPTER XV

Jewish laughter

Sometimes everything goes wrong, and finally things are in such a terrible mess that instead of crying we burst out laughing.

One morning you may get up late, and you are in a bad humor because you are being scolded, and you will be late for school. You can't find one of your shoes, and then when you go to breakfast you spill the milk and when you try to wipe it up, the glass falls on the floor and breaks. And when you lean over to pick up the pieces, you fall off the chair.

Instead of crying, you laugh.

Laughing in times of trouble

That is the way the Jews of the old world laughed. Life seemed very hard, so they learned to laugh. And even today we say that Jewish humor has a little spice of bitterness in it.

Whenever Jews have a great deal of trouble, their sense of humor helps them to live. Nowadays, we hear a great many jokes about Israel. When times were hardest in Israel, during the war,

there were new jokes every day. In a few hours, the new jokes passed from mouth to mouth across the little country. And people felt better. They could face the new day with a new joke.

In the old days in Europe, the Jews of the villages knew how to tell funny stories that made everybody laugh at their troubles.

Wise and foolish, rich and poor

The Hassidim believed that all life should be joyful, and they worshipped God with singing and with laughter. Their leaders often taught them religious ideas by spinning tales, and some of these tales were funny.

There would be stories of the wise man and the fool, showing how the wise man puzzled his head and worried himself and beat his brains to answer some riddle asked him by the King. And then the fool came along, and with God's help and a little luck, the fool gave the right answer.

Or there would be stories of the rich man and the poor man, showing how in the end the poor man laughed at the rich man, because the poor man had his health and his family, and the rich man had only gold.

This kind of story telling goes far back in Jewish life.

Stories from the Agada and Midrash

We already know that a part of the Talmud called the Agada is made up of tales. And there were still other stories made up by the rabbis. These were called "midrashim."

The Midrash has all kinds of stories, many of them funny tales. There are tales about heroes like David and about wise men like Moses, who is called Moshe Rabenu, Moses our teacher. There are tales about Solomon and his wisdom, and tales about Elijah, who suddenly appears out of nowhere to help people who are in danger.

The rabbis of old Europe knew these stories, and kept on adding to them, just as when you tell a story you sometimes add your own touches. And Jews kept on making up new stories, especially about Elijah, as though he were still going around playing pranks and helping people.

Elijah and the bear

For instance, there were stories about Elijah and the dance of the bears. Some of the Polish noblemen liked to play a cruel game. When they had big parties, they would amuse their guests by a bear's dance. Only, it would not be a real bear. They would seize a Jew, and dress him in a heavy bearskin. Then the nobleman or one of his serv-

ants cracked the whip, and the bear had to dance and keep on dancing for his life. The long whip cracked around him and the noblemen laughed.

So the Jews made up tales about the bear's dance. Just when the poor Jew was worn out, Elijah would come and take his place in the bearskin. And then Elijah would jump on the man with the whip, and beat him up.

Tales of the Maggidim

Such were the tales they told to keep up their spirits. Certain Jews were ex-

Chelmites trying to capture the moon

105

perts in telling these tales. Then there were certain traveling preachers called "Maggidim." The Maggid would go from town to town preaching in the synagogues. When a famous Maggid came to a town, it was a great event.

One of the best storytellers was the Maggid of Dubno. He seemed to know thousands of stories, and each story was exactly right for the moral of his sermon.

Once, a great scholar asked the Maggid of Dubno how he was able to find the right story for each moral. The Maggid said, "I'll answer about the story with a story."

The story of the sharpshooter

And the story he told was about a Polish landowner whose ambition was for his son to become the best sharpshooter in all Poland. He sent the boy to military school, and the boy became such a good shot that he won all the medals for marksmanship. On his way home, he stopped one night at a wayside inn kept by a Jew. While putting his horse in the stable, he noticed many bull's eye targets chalked on the wall. And in the very center of the tiny bull's eye of each target, there was a bullet hole.

The young nobelman was astonished at such marksmanship. He rushed into the tavern and asked the innkeeper, "Who is such a wonderful sharpshooter?"

"My son," said the innkeeper.

"Your son? It's impossible! How can a Jew shoot like that?"

"That's easy," said the innkeeper.

"First he shoots the bullet. Then he draws the bull's eye around the hole."

Yiddish "penny books"

Such tales began to be printed in little Yiddish story books, called penny books. Women loved to read these stories to their children.

As storytelling was the chief entertainment, there were always new stories. There were amusing Sabbath tales about travelers who got stuck on the road and had wild adventures, and there were tales about greedy persons who got fooled when they sought a big dowry in a marriage. There were tales about husbands and mothers-in-law and matchmakers.

Chelm: An imaginary town of fools

And there was one group of stories that had a very special flavor. These were yarns about an imaginary town, a town of fools, called Chelm. The Chelmites were always doing things in the most complicated way, like trying to trap the moon in a rainbarrel. Yet they somehow managed to get along, in spite of their foolish mistakes.

A number of the stories of Chelm were told as riddles. One Chelmite asks another, "What is more important, the sun or the moon?" The second answers, "The sun, of course." "Oh no," says the first one. "The moon is more important. The moon gives light when it's dark, and the sun only shines when it's light."

Another comical story of Chelm is about the man whose job was to go around knocking on the shutters every morning to wake people up. When he became very old it was hard for him to walk around the town. "I know," said a Chelmite, "Let's take down all the shutters and put them in his house. Then he can knock on them without walking all over town!"

Stories like this seem nonsensical, but yet they show us that life is sometimes upside-down. And then, comical stories can tell us much more. They can tell us not to be too proud of ourselves. They can remind us that some people seem born to have bad luck, so that even while we laugh at them, we feel friendly toward them.

Schlemiel and Schlimazel

For instance, a Chelmite was pretty close to a favorite Jewish character called a "schlemiel." A schlemiel never can do anything right. If you put him on a train, he loses his ticket. But he is not quite the same as a "schlimazel."

A schlimazel is always having bad luck, but not because of his own fault. An old Jewish story explains the difference between these two sad comical characters. "A schlemiel is a fellow who spills a bowl of hot soup on a schlimazel."

Sholom Aleichem, a famous writer

Soon there were favorite writers who turned some of these characters into literature. One of the most famous writers called himself Sholem Aleichem, the Hebrew phrase which means "peace unto you." Sholom Aleichem wrote a great many stories, books and plays about the old Jewish way of life.

At the time he lived, there was a great sweep of emigration from the Jewish towns and ghettoes of Europe, to

The "shtetl" or village of Eastern Europe, showing the small homes in which the Jews lived. Like the other buildings, the synagogue was made of wood, and was always the tallest building in the Jewish settlement.

America. Sholom Aleichem came to New York like the parents and grandparents of most of us. In America, his stories were translated. He wrote about how Jews from the old country learned to live in a new way—how "greenhorns" became Americans. One of his best books, which you can read in English, is about Motele, a little orphan boy who came to this country.

From the books of such writers, we get a taste of the bitter-sweet humor of the old communities in Europe. This helps us to understand the Jewish way of life as it was up to the time of our grandfathers.

A joke makes things even

But Jewish humor is very much a part of our own way of life. Some of the good Jewish jokes that were told in the days of our grandfathers, and before, are still told by famous comedians. That is because a really good joke is more than a joke. It has a meaning.

Usually a Jewish joke helps to balance things out, to make things even. The small man gets a laugh at the big, proud, over-important fellow. The poor man gets a laugh at the rich man. Even the scholar, who thinks he knows everything, is taken down a peg.

Here is a simple example of how a Jewish joke makes the small man equal to the big man, by reminding us that much for which we take credit is really God's gift:

A very famous cantor comes to sing for the holidays. His wife is very conceited about him and she brags to one of the women of the congregation, "Isn't he wonderful! He's famous all over the world!"

"What's so wonderful about him?" says the other woman. "If my husband had his voice, he could sing just as well!"

Bringing joy to others

The Jewish ability to make jokes, to take even the worst tragedy with humor, reminds us that Jews believe that life is good. We believe we should seek joy wherever we can in life, and try to bring joy to others, if only by a good laugh.

THINKING ABOUT WHAT YOU HAVE LEARNED

1. Can you tell any Midrashic stories about Biblical heroes?
2. How does Jewish humor help us to understand some important Jewish ideas about life? Why do we laugh at the famous Chelm stories?

QUESTIONS TO ASK YOUR PARENTS

1. Yiddish humor has given us many words which are widely used by American Jews and non-Jews: kibbitz, schlemiel, schlimazel. Ask your parents if they remember any stories in which such words are used.
2. Does this chapter in Jewish humor help to explain why so many Jews in America have become famous comedians?

The Jewish Way of Life under freedom

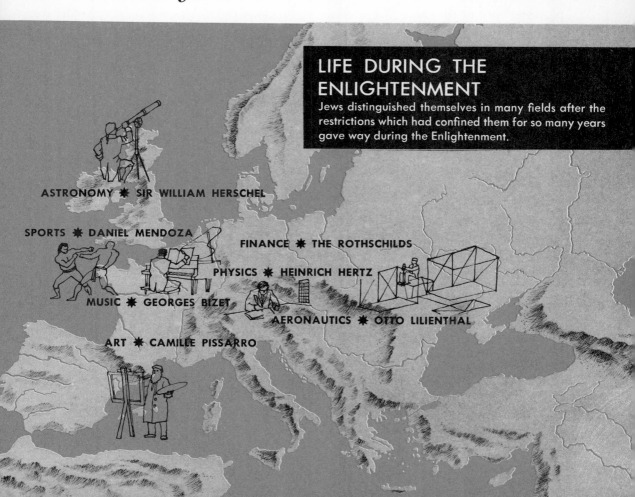

LIFE DURING THE ENLIGHTENMENT

Jews distinguished themselves in many fields after the restrictions which had confined them for so many years gave way during the Enlightenment.

ASTRONOMY ✳ SIR WILLIAM HERSCHEL

SPORTS ✳ DANIEL MENDOZA

FINANCE ✳ THE ROTHSCHILDS

PHYSICS ✳ HEINRICH HERTZ

MUSIC ✳ GEORGES BIZET

AERONAUTICS ✳ OTTO LILIENTHAL

ART ✳ CAMILLE PISSARRO

CHAPTER XVI

The Jews seek freedom

We keep saying that the Jews had an old-time way of life, and that now they live in a different way. How did the change come about? Was it because so many Jews moved from Europe to America and found that in America life was different?

Change started in Europe

It was more than that. The change had already begun a long time ago, in Europe itself. It began in England and France and Germany and, some years later, in Russia, Poland and the eastern part of Europe. The Jews began to move out of the ghettos and to study other things than the Talmud and the Torah. A change came, not only in the lives of the Jews, but in the lives of other people.

This change in the ways of the world is still spreading. It is reaching the backward and the oppressed people of the earth. This change has many important ideas. But the most important idea is the change from rulers to the idea of freedom and equality for the people.

We all know that in the old days, kings and nobles ruled. Some rulers were kind and some were cruel, but all the people worked for them and most of the people were poor and ignorant. The kings and noblemen made their own laws and the people had to obey, because the noblemen owned most of the land on which the people lived.

How the change began

In many countries there were special laws for Jews. They had even fewer rights than the other subjects, and so many of them joined the fight for freedom.

Slowly, over hundreds of years, things had been changing. Printing had been invented and, because of this, more people had learned to read, more people had books and more people got ideas. They got ideas that it wasn't right for only the kings and nobles to own all the land and to rule. They got ideas that everybody ought to have a say-so in the government.

First, there were peasants who rebelled against giving most of their crops to the nobles and kings. They wanted to have their own land and keep what they grew. Then there were people in the town, merchants and craftsmen, who demanded a say-so. In France and in England there were writers and leaders who declared that kings were not holy and that ordinary people should have a say-so in their government.

Finding freedom in America

When a new land like America was discovered, people went to the new land. And there they were free to make a life for themselves. When the British king tried to rule the American colonists, for example, the colonists said no and rebelled. They said they would make their own government.

They fought against the rulers who sent armies from the old countries, and they defeated them. And they made their own government, our government, saying that all men are created equal and that everyone has a right to life, liberty and the pursuit of happiness.

"Everybody" means the Jews, too. Already in America the Jews had been mingling more freely than had been allowed in some of the countries of Europe. They had been working at all kinds of occupations. They had gone out to trade with the Indians; they had sailed trading ships; they had worked as diggers and builders. They had pleaded in the courts as lawyers, and some of them had started plantations. And as they mingled freely with all sorts of people, their way of life began to change.

A Jewish trader to the Indians in colonial America

French Revolution gave rights to Jews

France was a country in which many ideas of freedom grew. There was a revolution in France in 1789, a few years after the American Revolution. The French king was overthrown, and France became a free country with the slogan, "Liberty, Equality, Fraternity" for all. Soon afterward, Jews were given rights as citizens.

When Napoleon was the leader of France, he became a new kind of ruler. And even though he went out with his armies and for a time conquered many lands—Germany, Austria, Italy, Spain—he brought new laws of freedom to those countries. The ghettos were opened. Jews were allowed to live outside of ghettos. Some were allowed to go to colleges where they had once been forbidden. In these colleges they began to study other knowledge besides their own Talmud.

Jews were allowed to work in occupations that had been forbidden to them. And as they entered the outside world they began to take a part in the fight for freedom that was going on in so many lands. And as the Jews in each country helped the people fight for more freedom, the Jews began to ask for the same rights as everyone else—the right to own land, to vote, to worship freely, and the right to bear arms. For in some countries the Jews had even been forbidden to join the army.

The people whom they were helping to gain freedom, in their turn wanted to help the Jews. In America, as democracy and liberty were won, the Jews gained their rights and kept them. But in other lands where the government went back and forth between the new and old ways, the Jews sometimes gained rights, then lost them and had to struggle to win them again.

Changes came faster in some lands

But through all this time, which took several generations, the ways of the Jews kept changing. Their ways were not changing with the same speed in all countries. In Poland and Russia, for instance, the old ways hung on. In Germany and in France and in England, the new ways came more quickly. And in America, the new country, they came quickest of all.

Germany was one of the countries where the treatment of the Jews went back and forth from bad to good to bad again. The story of Jewish life in Germany proves how people must always stay on the alert to keep their freedom. Even after they have won some rights, they must be ready to struggle to keep their rights.

We all know that during World War II the most horrible crimes in history were done to the Jews by the Germans. Waves of evil came over the entire country, the entire people.

And yet we have to remember that at other times the Germans behaved like good people. We have to remember that even though Germany under Hitler was terrible for the Jews, it was actually in that same country that the first important movement of freedom and enlightenment for the Jews was started.

Jews had been living in Germany long before Germany was a kingdom. Back

The Crusaders attacked Jewish communities

in the Middle Ages, the land along the Rhine River was divided up among different dukes and princes, each ruling a small kingdom. They had not yet joined together to make the large kingdom of Germany. The Jews were helpful as traders between these small kingdoms, and many of the Jewish communities along the Rhine were prosperous. There were famous Jewish scholars and doctors in those communities.

Jews fled from Germany during the Crusades

Then as the Middle Ages ended, there came a very bitter time, the time of the Crusaders. The Crusaders gathered armies in Europe to go to Palestine to drive out the Muslims who ruled the Holy Land at that time.

But while the Crusaders were marching across Europe to go to the Holy Land, they attacked Jewish communities. They burned and killed many Jews.

To save their lives, large numbers of 113

Jewish families fled to Poland and to Russia, where they settled. In the previous unit, we studied how their way of life grew. After the Crusaders had passed on their way, Jews were allowed to resume their lives. But new laws had been passed. Jews now had to wear yellow badges to show that they were Jews. This was also what Hitler made them do hundreds of years later.

In the time of the Crusaders, the Jews also had to pay heavy taxes and fines. They were driven out of many occupations. In some of the small kingdoms, only one boy from each Jewish family could get permission to marry. The reason for this was that there was so little room in the ghetto for new families.

Moses Mendelssohn comes to Berlin

But the Jews struggled to win back their rights. Sometimes they found friendly rulers, and sometimes they bought back their rights at great cost. Slowly, the Jews returned to the places from which they had been driven. One of these cities was Berlin.

At first, only doctors and lawyers and wealthy merchants were given permission to live in the city of Berlin. After some time, these Jews won the right to have a synagogue. They did not have a rabbi in the city, so they sent to the town of Dessau and invited a well-known scholar, Rabbi Fraenkel, to come and be rabbi of Berlin.

In Dessau, Rabbi Fraenkel had a bright pupil whose name was Moses Mendelssohn.

Young Moses Mendelssohn begged to be allowed to follow his teacher to Berlin. It was not easy for a Jew who was

a mere student to get a permit to live in that city, but because he was so bright, he finally won a permit in 1743.

Now, up to that time, Moses Mendelssohn had studied only the Talmud and other books of the Jewish world. But already in those days a new kind of education was in the air. The movement called the Enlightenment was on the way.

This was a movement for Jews to study subjects that were outside of the Jewish books of religion. It was a movement to study all knowledge, especially history and philosophy. Everywhere in Europe, not only the Jews, but all people struggling for freedom, felt their brains stirring. They wanted to read, to study, to know.

You can imagine how it was in those days, if you think about the study of the atom today. Only a few years ago we knew very little about the atom. And today the way has been opened and everyone is rushing to find out more and more. So people are more interested than ever in learning about the planets and the stars and the universe.

Just as we are excited and eager to learn about the atom, so the Jews were eager for the new education. Moses Mendelssohn began to read books in the German language, books that were outside the circle of Jewish knowledge. And he said, "Why shouldn't Jews study all of these new sciences as well as their Talmud?"

Mendelssohn learned to write in German

Besides his Jewish studies with Rabbi Fraenkel, Moses Mendelssohn studied world history and philosophy. He began

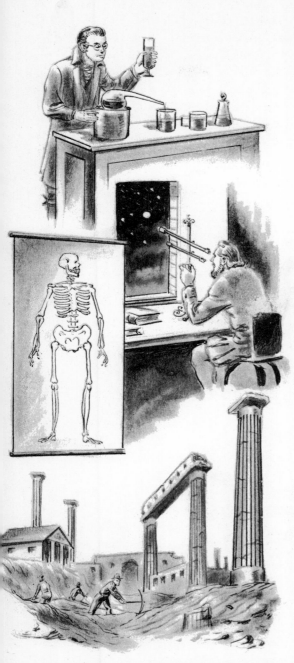

The Enlightenment expanded all knowledge

to write in German, too. He became a leading philosopher and soon he was quite famous among German writers.

It may seem strange to us today to realize that the students in the colleges of those days didn't know what Jews were like. Nobody believed that Jews would write and think and make scientific experiments. With Moses Mendelssohn they began to see that this could be.

Mendelssohn decided that the way should be opened for Jews to come to the knowledge of the world. It was only sensible for Jews to be part of the life of the country they lived in. They could keep their Jewish faith, and still be active citizens of their land. But the Jews had been kept apart for so long —how could the Jews and the German people get to know each other?

Mendelssohn became a scholar-hero

First, he decided, more Jews had to learn to read and write in German. So he began to translate the Bible into German, because it would be easy for Jews who knew the Book so well to learn German by reading the Bible in that language. He hoped that after they read the Bible in German, the Jews would go on to read other German books, to learn the culture of the Germans among whom they lived. Finally, they could become full citizens, while remaining good Jews.

Some famous German writers who believed that all men should have equal rights joined Moses Mendelssohn in his work. Moses Mendelssohn became a kind of scholar-hero. An important German author named Lessing wrote a play with Mendelssohn as the hero, called "Nathan the Wise."

Mendelssohn was not trying to make the Jews forget the Talmud or forget that they were Jews. He was trying to broaden their ideas, to bring them into the modern world of Enlightenment where modern science and ideas were being born.

At the same time, he himself observed all the laws of Judaism, all the religious customs. And he urged others to do the same. Yet the movement that he had started was bound to change many things in the daily lives of a great many Jews, and we shall see how the changes came about.

THINKING ABOUT WHAT YOU HAVE LEARNED

1. How did Moses Mendelssohn hope to help Jews in Germany learn the German language?
2. Explain how the invention of the printing press led to more rights for the Jews.

QUESTIONS TO ASK YOUR PARENTS

1. What happened in Germany in modern times to remind us of the days of the Crusades in that country?
2. Why did the modern ideas of freedom develop faster in America than they did in Europe?

James Watt's early steam engine

CHAPTER XVII

The Jewish Way of Life changes with freedom

Perhaps you have a big brother or sister who went away to college and came back home for vacation and wanted to change everything around the house. "That's not the way that we do things at college," they say. So they may want different kinds of food at the table, or they may have different ideas about how the house should be decorated.

Then your parents say, "Our house has always been this way, and it's the way we like it, and the way we want to keep it." Then there is an argument. In the end, some of the new ideas are used in the house, and often the college boys and girls may decide they still like many of the old-fashioned ideas, too, because they feel more at home with them.

Now something like this happened, only in a bigger way, after Moses Mendelssohn and other Jews started to read books that were outside their old way of life. After a number of Jews came to live in cities like Berlin and to find that they were free to go anywhere, they wanted to change their lives at home.

Enlightenment and emancipation

First, there was the word "enlightenment." The new kind of reading and education was like a bright light that showed them much of the world they had never seen before. This was called "enlightenment." Then came emancipation. What is "emancipation"? You may have heard that word already, because it is the word used by Abraham Lincoln when he freed the slaves. He freed them by making an Emancipation Proclamation. That is, he proclaimed them to be emancipated, or free.

The Jews who were freed from the ghetto and who studied modern knowledge called themselves emancipated. As they mingled with the rest of the population, many Jews felt that they ought to dress more like everyone else. And some of the Jews cut off their earlocks and beards. They said that they could give up their old-fashioned clothes and some of their strict customs without giving up the main ideas of Judaism. These ideas, the love of God, the love of justice and charity, could be kept even if the *117* regulations about what to eat and what not to eat were not always strictly kept.

Some of the German Jews argued that the regulations that had grown more and more complicated through the centuries were not even the regulations of the Books of Moses in the Bible. They pointed out that the kind of clothing the Jews wore did not belong to the Holy Land in the Biblical days, but to the Middle Ages and to Poland. Why cling to such old customs and ceremonies?

They felt that what was needed was a more modern way for Jews to live as Jews in their new freedom. And that is how a number of changes came about, leading to ways of Jewish life that we have today. Of course a large number of Jews kept on feeling that the old ways were the right ways.

Using German in the synagogue

As you remember, the Yiddish language began with German hundreds of years ago. But in those years, many Russian and Polish words had been added to Yiddish, so that to a German it only sounded like very bad German. Educated people in Germany hated to hear this and educated German Jews did not want to speak Yiddish.

Israel Jacobson founded a school in Cassel where Bible stories were taught to the children of these emancipated

Jews and non-Jews mingled freely

Jews. As the children did not know Hebrew, he said they should be taught in German and that the service should be explained in German. Then he decided to hold a children's service in the German language, just as we have it in English.

This was a new idea! Until then the services were entirely in Hebrew. The parents of these children were pleased with this idea, and Jacobson arranged the same kind of service for them. Many of the Hebrew prayers were translated into German, and a sermon was preached in German.

These were the first important changes in Jewish worship because of the Age of Enlightenment. Today, when we go to services in a reform or conservative synagogue and find part of the service in English, we can think back to the time when children heard their service in German for the first time.

Israel Jacobson and his students

Equal rights for women

Another part of emancipation was to give more rights to women. In Jewish life, too, there was a movement for women to have more rights. And so women came to have a better place in the synagogue. They sat together with the men. Girls were given a religious education, just the same as boys. And when they finished their synagogue school, both the girls and the boys had a confirmation service.

More changes in the services

Once these Jews began to make changes, they made all sorts of changes in the synagogue service. To those who ob-jected, they pointed out that changes had been made all along in the history of the Jews. After all, the services described in the Bible tell us of animal sacrifices made by priests on the altars of the Temple in Jerusalem. For hundreds of years there have been no such services in the Jewish religion. And they said that what has been changed once can be changed again, as long as the spiritual idea of Judaism is kept whole.

In the old synagogues, the cantor sang but there were no instruments. The changing congregations of Germany decided that they would have organ music during the service. They wanted to make religious worship more beautiful.

119

Some Jews thought that this was only an imitation of churches where organ music is played, but the emancipated Jews said they were really going back to the Bible for their inspiration. In the Bible we are told how King David played on his harp when he sang his prayers to God. There was a whole orchestra of instruments in the Temple of old. Why, then, shouldn't there be a musical instrument in the synagogue?

In the changing congregations, the prayers were examined to see whether they applied to the new kind of life. And some changes were made so that the ideas of the prayers should fit when applied to modern times. For instance, there were the prayers for the coming of Messiah to lead all Jews back to Palestine where they would rebuild the Temple.

There were enlightened Jews who said that Messiah was not a person but an idea, and that rebuilding the Temple did not necessarily mean to put up an actual building in Jerusalem. Instead,

CONSERVATIVE

ORTHODOX

REFORM

The three major Jewish groups in America

it meant the building up of the ideas of truth and justice and love of God.

They said that if the ideas of peace and goodness were spread over the earth, then it was as if Messiah had come. They said that if people lived a good religious life, then the Temple was wherever they lived, in Germany, in America, in Russia or in Palestine.

Arguments about the prayers

To change the order of the Sabbath prayers brought violent arguments in the Jewish world. Scholars who studied ancient Jewish history said that Jews had always had the right to change their prayers and their worship service. A famous historian, Leopold Zunz, reminded the Jews that it was only after they had been shut up in ghettos that they had become afraid to change anything, and had made their rules so very strict.

But there were equal numbers who said that God's word had been revealed once and for all to Moses on Mount Sinai. They said religious rules could never be changed.

The orthodox rabbis urged all Jews to cling to the age-old traditions. The leader of this group was Rabbi Samson Raphael Hirsch. He and his followers declared that a Jew could live in the new free world and be an orthodox observer. He could live as a modern man and retain all the customs of his fathers.

Some took the middle way

You know that when two groups take opposite sides in an argument, there are always some who want to find a middle way. They see some good ideas on both sides. So when an argument grew between the orthodox and the liberal Jews, there was a group that tried to find a middle way. They were what we would call today conservative Jews because they wanted to change but they also wanted to conserve the traditions. Their leader was Rabbi Zacharias Frankel.

Rabbi Frankel said it was true there had always been changes made in Jewish worship. But he said these changes should come gradually, as reinterpretations of Jewish law.

So the conservative Jews kept many of the prayers in the Hebrew language, but they had their sermon in German so everyone could understand. They agreed with the orthodox Jews about keeping the Messianic prayer for the return to Palestine. But they agreed with the reform Jews about men and women sitting together. When it came to organ music, they left the decision up to each congregation.

All agree on the fundamentals

So from these days in Germany, there came to be three synagogue groups in Jewish life—the orthodox, the reform and the conservative. In the United States, the three groups are almost equal to each other in membership. And though their ways of worship are not quite the same, the three Jewish groups agree on the deeper things.

They agree on the worship of One God, on the importance of the Bible, on the need to observe Sabbath and the holidays. They agree on the value of being a Jew, on the Ten Commandments and on all the great laws urging Jews to live by what is right and what is good in dealing with their fellow men.

Through these three main groups it is possible for every Jew to find a way of life that suits him. In each, the synagogue remains the center of his activity, the gathering place of his community. By showing that it is able to change with new times and yet remain the same in its true meaning, Judaism proved itself to be the life of the Jewish people.

THINKING ABOUT WHAT YOU HAVE LEARNED

1. What do the words "enlightenment" and "emancipation" tell us about the life of the Jews at the end of the 18th century?
2. Explain the important ideas for which the following four men stand in modern Jewish history—Israel Jacobson; Leopold Zunz; Samson Raphael Hirsch; and Zacharias Frankel.

QUESTIONS TO ASK YOUR PARENTS

1. Why was there a new emphasis on equal rights for women in synagogue worship and in education?
2. When a new congregation is organized in a community, which beliefs and practices determine whether it is Reform, Orthodox, or Conservative?

CHAPTER XVIII

New Ways of helping Jews in need

When the Jews were allowed to live in many of Europe's big cities, and as they left the ghettos, some of them became rich. In some cities they still were not allowed to work in every trade. But one kind of business was open to the Jews. This was moneylending or banking. In fact, in some countries, the Jews were forced to be moneylenders, because the noblemen needed money and refused to allow the Jews to live in their lands unless they provided the loans.

The grand dukes and princes and rulers of some of the small kingdoms did not want to bother their heads with financial problems. Each would leave these problems to an expert, often a Jew, who became known as "his Jew." Thus a few Jews were able to rise to positions of importance in the courts of Europe.

The noblemen were often gamblers who wasted their money, and they would come to the Jews to pawn their jewels, demanding big loans. In this way, many of the important Jewish families of today got their start by lending money. As their loan business grew, they became bankers. Others became wealthy merchants, or what we would call wholesale traders. And still others became manufacturers.

Mayer Rothschild and his five sons

Among the wealthy Jews, almost the first name anyone thinks of is Rothschild. In German, this name means Red Shield, and it comes from the house in Frankfort, Germany, where the founder of this family fortune was born. His name was Mayer, and the little house in the ghetto where his parents lived had a red shield on it.

When Mayer grew up and became a money lender, people who had to find him said, "Mayer of the red shield," and soon he was called Mayer Rothschild.

Mayer Rothschild had five sons, and they went to different countries to open branches of his banking business. One went to France and one went to England, and soon there were Rothschilds in America, too. This made it possible for their banking business to grow, since the brothers could trust each other and *123* could keep in close touch with information about business conditions in each country.

Charity on a big scale

In the old way of life in the ghetto, you remember that the care of the needy was part of the daily life of the whole community. There were collection boxes in every house and there were people in the community who gave their time to help the needy. But as Jews began to scatter, living sometimes outside the ghetto, there were needs that could not be taken care of by the next door neighbors.

More important than this, there were times when entire communities of Jews were destroyed by pogroms and tremendous sums were needed for relief.

And so such people as Moses Montefiore and the Rothschild family and other wealthy Jewish families began to think of charity in bigger ways. The idea came not only to give people food and clothing, but to set them up in a new life, sometimes in a new country, so that they could earn their own living.

The Rothschild family in France was headed by Baron Edmund de Rothschild. When there were dreadful pogroms against Jews in Russia, the French Baron grew interested in plans to build a new Jewish community in Palestine. "Let us take the Jews out of Russia, where they are in danger," he said, "and let us give them a new start in the old land."

Now this was not the idea of a Messiah who would lead all the Jews back to Palestine. This was an idea of an emancipated Jew, educated in the ways of the non-Jewish world, but still a very loyal Jew. The Baron sent his organizers to Palestine with large sums of money. Their job was to buy land and start new villages, so that Jews who were fleeing from the Russian pogroms could settle in Palestine and earn their living as farmers.

Some of the Baron's colonies are flourishing towns in Israel today. This was one of the earliest examples in the world of the new kind of charity called philanthropy which means "love of people." It meant a planned program of helping many people to get on their feet to earn their own living, instead of giving them a day-to-day ration of food. But we know that this idea is not new to the

Buying land from a Turk

Jews. It is the highest of the eight degrees of tzedakah of Maimonides, centuries before Rothschild.

Baron de Hirsch helps Jews in America

In the terrible days of the pogroms, the Russian Jews were helped by another great Jewish millionaire whose name was Baron de Hirsch. His idea, too, was to help the Jews to move out of the land of pogroms. But instead of bringing them to Palestine, where farming was not easy, he chose the American continent.

Baron de Hirsch spent over a hundred million dollars in helping Jews to leave Russia to come and settle in North or South America. Since few of the Jews from the old country had been allowed to become farmers, Baron de Hirsch started a farming school in the United States for them. He also financed the Jewish Agricultural Society. Even today, the funds set up by Baron de Hirsch are in operation, helping Jews to settle on farms. Many refugees from Hitler's slave camps have been settled on farms in New Jersey through the aid of the Jewish Agricultural Society.

As Jews came to the new lands, some of them in their turn became prosperous. And these Jews, too, as they were taught by their religion, gave a large part of their fortunes to philanthropy.

But even while Jewish philanthropy became organized in a big way, the col- 125 lection boxes were still to be seen in many Jewish homes. Today, your parents probably give their charity in checks, and they may keep a collection box in the house only for the pennies and nickels of the children. The Jews of America have been fortunate, so that there are fewer among them who need help than there were among the Jews of Europe. But Jewish schools and centers and congregations always need money for their work, and there are the needs of Jews in the rest of the world.

In a ghetto community, if the milkman's daughters had no dowry, all the women of the little town worried about it and tried to collect money to help the girls get married. But today we need to collect very large sums so that the Jews of Israel may take in refugees. We need to collect large sums to build synagogues and temples where you can learn about your religion and where you can have many activities.

Tzedakah in today's Jewish community

So even though our daily way of life has changed, our belief in our responsibility to help each other is just as strong as ever. And instead of carrying out this work by direct personal contact, we carry it out through group organizations.

If you watch the activity around you in the Jewish community, you will see that the daily life of the Jew is still very much occupied with tzedakah.

There are meetings and bazaars and dinners and shows, all arranged to raise funds for the big Jewish organizations that help needy persons all over the

Learning a trade in an ORT school

126

world. There are U.J.A. drives in every Jewish community every year. This is the United Jewish Appeal that raises funds to help Jews everywhere.

Through the Joint Distribution Committee, the U.J.A. sends teams of workers wherever there are Jews in need. It sends medical supplies and nurses and teachers to the backward countries of North Africa, where tens of thousands of Jews live in slums. Medical help is given not only to Jews, but to their neighbors. It helps refugees to America to establish new homes.

There is the ORT, the Organization for Rehabilitation Through Training, which maintains schools in backward countries to teach trades to young people, so they may be able to earn their own living. There is the Histadruth organization for Jewish labor in Israel; and there is the Hadassah, the women's organization for medical care and Youth Aliyah in Israel. There is the Council of Jewish Women. There is the Hebrew Immigrant Aid Society. And there are countless other groups, all doing their part to help their fellow Jews.

There are also drives for the Hebrew University and the Technion, in Israel, and for Brandeis University in this country. And there are the federation drives and the Community Chest drives for all our local needs. With all these activities, tzedakah indeed remains a way of life for the American Jew.

THINKING ABOUT WHAT YOU HAVE LEARNED

1. The Jews who fled from the pogroms in Russia were helped by two famous French Jews who had the title of "Baron." Who were they and what did they accomplish?
2. How did it happen that Jews like Rothschild became wealthy as bankers?

QUESTIONS TO ASK YOUR PARENTS

1. Which Jewish philanthropic organization do your parents support?
2. Which Jews in your community have won the greatest recognition as philanthropists?

CHAPTER XIX

The Jews seek justice under freedom

Sometimes it takes more than money to help people who are in trouble. People may need a great deal of help to obtain justice. For they may find themselves victimized by hatred and prejudice. Or they may be falsely accused of a crime.

Jews believe in human rights

To fight for human rights is part of every Jew's basic belief. Our Prophets raised their voices in every marketplace in the Holy Land and in the palace of the King. And when they were imprisoned for pleading social justice, they cried out from the dungeons. They raised their voices to utter the words of God, for they were God-inspired to struggle for justice, and they told the people, "Thus spake the Lord our God."

And through the ages, because of this prophetic tradition, Jews have fought for justice and joined others in this struggle for liberty. In Germany in 1848, when the people tried to win democratic rights, Jews were among the leaders. In Russia in 1905, when the people tried to break the iron rule of the Czars, Jews were among the leaders.

Today in our own country, in every struggle against prejudice and against censorship, Jews take their part and more than their part. They take their part as individuals and also in groups. Our rabbis and Jewish leaders speak out against every form of injustice. We engage in this struggle because we know from the sad experiences of our own people that injustice is a terrible thing.

Sometimes people are accused of crimes only because they belong to a group against which hatred has been aroused. This has often happened to the Jews in the past.

In the law courts we are very careful when someone is accused of a crime. Our rule is that a man is innocent until he is proven guilty. And our courts make sure that every accused person has a lawyer to defend him. If he cannot afford to pay a lawyer, the court appoints a lawyer to help him free of charge.

But in the old days, in many countries

there were no such protections. A man could be accused of a crime and arrested and tortured until he said he did it, even if he had not done so. And in the old days this kind of torture was often used against Jews.

Superstitions about the Jewish religion

In many countries there were superstitious people who made up dreadful stories about the Jews. Today the whole civilized world knows that these stories were lies made up by evil and ignorant, and even insane, people. But it took a hard battle to show that these superstitions were lies.

The worst of the evil superstitions that had to be fought were about the Jewish religion. As you know, if you think someone has a secret, you try to guess what that secret might be, and you make up your own ideas of that secret. Usually you imagine it to be as bad as possible. You imagine the secret is some dreadful thing.

And that is how people started imagining things against the Jews. They imagined that the Jewish religion had secrets. Because the Jews worshipped in a strange language, the people around them imagined that magical incantations were taking place. And then they thought of a terrible idea. They imagined that Jews used blood for religious ceremonies. Sometimes it was said that Jews killed non-Jews and used their blood in baking matzoh for Passover.

Another terrible story was that Jews poisoned wells. This was widely believed because Jews did not seem to die of some of the plagues that spread in those days. There was a "black plague" in Europe during the 14th century that killed thousands of people. But in some places, the Jews did not catch it because they were protected by their religious rules of cleanliness and because they were separated by ghetto walls from the rest of the population.

The Black Death

Wild stories led to pogroms

In those days people did not know about germs. They did not know why some Jews escaped the disease. So they said the disease was a Jewish plot. They said that the Jews poisoned the wells and then stayed away from them so that only non-Jews would catch the plague. Often such wild stories led to pogroms in which entire Jewish communities were destroyed.

As people in England and France and America became better educated, these superstitious ideas were proven to be only tales coming from hatred and from wild imagination. And as the Jews in the modern countries became free, they were able to defend the Jews in the backward countries against such awful accusations. The help came through bringing such cases to the attention of the civilized world so that the world would cry, "Shame!"

In some of the civilized countries there were Jews who took an important part in the government, and they were able to go to the rulers of the backward countries and plead with them to stop the barbarian tortures.

Damascus case aroused Jews of the world

For example, there was a famous case about a century ago in the city of Damascus under Turkish rule. The case began when a priest in that city disappeared. It was learned that he had had a terrible argument with a mule driver, who said he would kill him. But instead of the mule driver, some innocent Jews

PETITIONS

LEGAL AID

were arrested and accused of murdering the priest.

One of these Jews was tortured so long and so terribly that he finally said he committed the crime, though of course he had not done it. But this one victim was not enough for the Jew-haters. They arrested seven leaders of the Jewish community in Damascus. All seven were tortured. Some of them "confessed." But three of them who were rabbis did not break down under torture.

The story of what was happening in Damascus was printed in newspapers all over the world, and civilized people began to protest. They said it was madness to imagine that Jews would kill a priest. Important Jews in England and France began to worry about the case.

RESEARCH

IMMIGRATION

CONSULTATION WITH PUBLIC OFFICIALS

Sir Moses Montefiore uses his influence

In England, there was a Jewish banker named Moses Montefiore. Like the Rothschilds, he was a great philanthropist. He performed many services for the English government and was elected sheriff of London. He was made a knight, Sir Moses Montefiore.

Sir Moses gave money to Jewish causes, such as building old-age homes in Jerusalem. But he also believed in the other kind of help, in using his influence to aid innocent Jews who were in trouble.

Through the hard work of Sir Moses and others, the English became interested in the Damascus case. The House of Parliament sent a message to the governor of Damascus asking for fair treatment for the Jews. And the American Ambassador in England joined in this protest.

Then Sir Moses Montefiore himself went to Turkey to see the Sultan. With Sir Moses went a French Jew, a lawyer and statesman named Adolph Cremieux.

The French Jew and the English Jew were able to show the Sultan that the Jews were innocent. They proved that the confessions came only as the result of torture. The Sultan set free the Damascus Jews and proclaimed to all his people that it was a lie to say that Jews used blood for religious purposes.

This was one of the important cases that set an example to the world. It helped stop the false charge of the blood ritual. But superstition is not easily stamped out. This horrible story came up again and again, in Russia and in Roumania and in other countries.

Montefiore in Russia and Palestine

Sir Moses Montefiore made many voyages to help Jews who were in trouble. He went twice to Russia. He was able to obtain audiences with kings and sultans and often his talks with rulers had good results.

Sir Moses was also very active in the first settlements of Jews in Palestine. He visited the country seven times. And his philanthropy was known in England, too. He gave money to hospitals and schools. And privately he made gifts to Jewish scholars and to widows and orphans.

One of his habits was to celebrate his birthday by giving instead of receiving presents. On each birthday, he made larger donations than before. It is an old Jewish custom to say, "May you live to be a hundred and twenty years old." People were always saying this to Sir Moses, and he actually lived to be a hundred and one years old! Many Jews felt that the blessings they had wished for him for his good deeds had come true.

Cases in Russia, Roumania and Switzerland

Adolph Cremieux of France was not a great millionaire. But he was untiring in his work to save the Jews. As he was a great lawyer, he used his talent for this purpose. Like Sir Moses, Adolph Cremieux visited Russia to help a Jew who was accused of a ritual murder. And the defense of the great French lawyer made the case famous all over the world.

He went to Roumania to plead with the government to grant rights to Jews who lived there. And he took up the case of Jews in Switzerland who had been ordered to leave the country. Cremieux went to his own government, the French government, and pleaded that they should denounce the action of the Swiss. He pleaded with the French government to break off diplomatic relations with a nation that still behaved in the uncivilized way of the Middle Ages.

Organizations to defend Jewish rights

Both Sir Moses and Cremieux started another important plan for helping their people. They agreed that help should not depend on any one person, no matter how rich or how kind he was. So both of them started groups who would watch out for the rights of Jews all over the world. Sir Moses started such an organization in England and Adolph Cremieux started one in France.

The Alliance Israelite Universelle of France is still very active today, not only in bringing help to those who are unjustly accused of crimes, but in building schools and spreading education in the backward areas of the world.

And in the United States, too, such groups have been formed. For example, we have the American Jewish Committee. Its representatives go to all parts of the world to help Jews who are suffering from evil attacks.

We have also the B'nai B'rith, which has members in every community. It maintains the Anti-Defamation League. Whenever lies are printed about Jews or others, whenever people are attacked because of their faith or creed, the Anti-Defamation League takes steps to stop such evil. But it does more than that. It makes scientific studies about how lies are spread and about how prejudice grows, so that we can learn how to prevent these things.

And then there is the American Jewish Congress, which is part of the World Jewish Congress, an organization that has members in all parts of the world. The Jewish Congress works to protect human rights everywhere.

All these organizations work for the same purpose as the Human Rights Commission of the United Nations, for the whole civilized world now understands that we must work together to put an end to racial hatred.

The Jewish faith has always commanded us to seek justice, just as it has always commanded us to be charitable. And every good Jew, whether orthodox or reform or conservative, and whether he is rich or poor, takes part in the fight for human rights.

THINKING ABOUT WHAT YOU HAVE LEARNED

1. What protections do we in America today have against such outrages as the Damascus Case?
2. What organizations defend the rights of Jews today and how do they go about it?

QUESTIONS TO ASK YOUR PARENTS

1. Are there any "superstitions" about Jews which are still heard today? How should you act if you heard these repeated?
2. Jewish organizations working for Jewish rights also try to help Negroes and other groups in America who have to fight for equal rights. Is this a good idea? Why?

The United Nations Building in New York

CHAPTER XX

How Jewish freedom was attacked

You may wonder why the Jews of Europe always were getting into such great trouble. Why did they have to flee from one country to another? Why were there burnings and robbings and the killing of Jews?

It is easy to blame someone different

The Jews were the easiest ones to blame when things went wrong. You know that in any group when things go wrong, the leader is likely to blame somebody. Somebody has to be the jinx. If you go out on a hike and lose your way, a mean leader will suddenly pick on somebody and claim he was the one who led the whole group in the wrong direction.

Whom will he pick on? Sometimes it will be someone who is small. Or else it might be a new kid who is not yet well known by the group. Or else it might be a kid who comes from a different place than the rest of you, and therefore "doesn't belong."

Anyway, the idea is to find someone to blame, and whoever is "different" is likely to get the blame for anything that

goes wrong. If your group knows how to play fair, of course this will not happen. You will not choose a leader who needs someone to blame. And all of you will be on the lookout for unfairness.

Grownups, and entire nations, can behave just like this. If a nation suffers from a famine or a plague or poverty, misguided rulers want someone to blame. Perhaps the rulers are spendthrifts, wasting the money of the people. Times get bad. They need someone to blame.

Jews suffered because they were "different"

And in such countries, the rulers almost always picked on the Jews, because the Jews were "different." Jews had their own religion. We have seen how legends and lies were spread about the Jewish religion.

Sometimes other groups get picked on, too. In the last three hundred years, the Puritans have been persecuted in England, the Quakers in England and in our own country, the Armenians in

Turkey, the Protestants in France, and the Catholics in our own country.

Jews were disliked for another reason, again unfair. It had to do with money. Since Jews were forbidden many kinds of work, they had become store keepers and traders and money lenders. They were used as tax collectors by the Polish noblemen. People always thought of themselves as paying money to Jews.

No matter how poor most of the Jews were, they seemed rich to those who bought things in Jewish stores or paid taxes to Jewish collectors. So it was easy for the peasants to be made to hate the Jews.

And so it happened that whenever there was trouble, whenever there was a famine or a plague or a war, people turned on the Jews.

That is how it happened that the Jews were attacked by the Cossacks. The Cossacks were ferocious horsemen who at that time were ruled by the Poles. And the Poles made their Jews collect taxes from the angry and rebellious Cossacks. When the Cossacks rose up in revolt against Polish rule, the first thing they did was to attack Jewish villages and burn them and murder the Jews. Such attacks even had a special name. They were called "pogroms."

Disease of anti-Semitism is contagious

And the strange hatred of the Jews that led to pogroms was like a disease with a name. It was called "anti-Semitism." And, like a disease, it seemed to be contagious. It spread.

Anti-Semitism was very bad in Russia and Poland, where pogroms kept taking place all the way up to World War I, in 1914. Most of the Jews of Europe lived in the area between Russia and Germany, and Russia and Germany were enemies in the war. So the fighting went back and forth across the area where the Jews lived. Jewish villages became a battleground. Families had to flee from their homes. The Jews of America sent food and medicine for these refugees, but still a great many of them perished because help could not reach them across the war-torn lands.

A Russian Jewish tax collector

135

Communists against anti-Semitism and religion

At the end of the First World War, there was a new government in Russia. The Czar was gone, and the Communists were in charge. The Communists said they did not believe in pogroms. They even made laws against anti-Semitism, agreeing that spreading hatred was a crime. For a few years, things were better.

But the Communists had other ideas about the Jews. The Communists were against all religions and they taught Jewish children to leave the religion of their people. They closed Jewish schools and stopped the printing of Jewish newspapers and magazines, thinking that the children would forget that they were Jews.

For a long time, this was not considered to be anti-Semitism. But now we see that killing the Jewish religion, and killing the Jewish culture, was Russia's slow way of trying to end the Jewish people.

"Scientific" anti-Semitism in Germany

Tragically, by the time of World War II, a quicker way of putting an end to the Jewish people had been thought of in Germany. A new kind of anti-Semitism had been born in that country. It was not the anti-Semitism of ignorant people. The new kind was called "scientific" anti-Semitism, and it was born amongst a people who were supposed to be educated. The new kind of anti-Semitism was spread by their leader, Adolf Hitler.

The Germans had lost the First World War and they felt bitter and beaten. For some years they were poor. And as you know, when people are in trouble they want to blame someone. So Hitler decided to blame the same old scapegoat, the Jewish people. But because the Germans were more educated than the Cossacks had been, the Germans had to be told a fancier kind of lie.

The big lie was that the Jews were all organized into a secret plot to rule the world. The Germans were told that the Jewish bankers, like the Rothschilds, had control of most of the money in the world, and that Jews secretly bribed the

rulers of France and England and America to make war on the Germans! They were also taught that the Germans were better than anyone else and were the "Master Race" and should rule the world.

The Germans believed Hitler's lies

These were big lies, of course, but Hitler thought that the bigger the lie and the more often you tell it, the more people will believe it. And many Germans believed it. Those who did not believe it were afraid to say "no" to Hitler because they would be thrown into a concentration camp. So Hitler and his

Nazis said they would kill all the Jews, so that then Germany could rule the world! They started the Second World War. And during the war, they conquered most of Europe and they killed nearly all the Jews that were there.

They did not kill them in fighting. The Jewish people who were trapped in Europe had no guns with which to fight. Even without weapons, they tried to resist the Germans, in such cities as Lodz and Vilna. And in the city of Warsaw the Jews put up a battle, against impossible odds, that is one of the most heroic stories in the history of the whole world.

137

Six million Jews exterminated

But little by little the Germans captured the Jews and sent them to concentration camps. There they were put to death in gas chambers. Six million Jews lost their lives in this way. Half of these were the Jews of Poland, for the Germans captured Poland at the beginning of the war. After that the Germans conquered France and Belgium and Hungary and Greece, and in each country they seized the Jews. The Jews of Germany itself had, of course, been the first to suffer.

Then the Germans invaded Russia. The Jews who lived in the battlefield part of Russia were also seized and murdered. So nearly three-fourths of all the Jews who lived in Europe were exterminated. That is perhaps the greatest tragedy in all of history.

Only those who were hidden by non-Jewish friends, or who fled outside the war zone, escaped. There were Jews who escaped to such countries as Sweden and America and England and Palestine.

And there were small numbers of Jews who joined groups of fighters in secret hideouts, from which they attacked the Germans. They were called partisans. These, too, were saved.

So the Jewish towns of Poland, and the great Jewish communities of Warsaw, Bialystok, Lodz and other cities, were destroyed. These were the communities from which many of our families had come when they sailed for America.

When those towns and cities were destroyed, the old-time Jewish way of life

had finally been stamped out by the Nazis.

After the war, Germany, where the movement of enlightenment had begun, was a land where almost no Jews lived or wanted to live. And nobody knew much about the Jews who remained

Jewish partisans sabotage a bridge

Little was known about what had happened to the famous Jewish communities in Moscow and Leningrad and Odessa. Once there had been many Jewish schools and theaters and newspapers and synagogues in those cities. Millions of Jews had been destroyed body and soul by the Germans. Now it was feared that millions more in Russia were being destroyed in their spirit.

New life in other lands

Yet the Jews as a people were finding new life in other parts of the world. The Jewish community in America had grown to five million—almost the size of the community destroyed in Europe. Here in our country the Jewish spirit was free and strong, new synagogues were being built, and schools and community centers and colleges of Jewish studies. Jewish thought was making its contribution to the new world.

And if the Jews in Europe had been crushed and their spirit stifled; and if the Enlightenment had not solved all the problems of the Jews—there was still hope. Hope was being reborn in Palestine. For after two thousand years the nation of Israel had again come to life in that land.

alive in Russia. For they had been cut off by the Iron Curtain from Jews in the free world. Although there were several million Jews in Russia, they were afraid even to write to their relatives on the other side of the Iron Curtain.

THINKING ABOUT WHAT YOU HAVE LEARNED

1. Can you describe a time when someone in your group who was "different" was blamed for something?
2. Why did the Cossacks attack the Jews in Poland?

QUESTIONS TO ASK YOUR PARENTS

1. How did Hitler and his Nazi party change the course of Jewish history in Europe?
2. What have been the effects of Communists rule on the Jews of Russia?

UNIT FIVE

The Jewish Way of Life in Israel

EUROPE 388,530

ASIA & AUSTRALIA 260,169

NORTH & SOUTH AMERICA 10,326

AFRICA 224,543

LEBANON

SYRIA

Haifa

SEA OF GALILEE

JORDAN RIVER

Tel Aviv

Jerusalem

DEAD SEA

SUEZ CANAL

EGYPT

Beersheba

JORDAN

NEGEV

Elath

IMMIGRATION TO ISRAEL
1948-1958

CHAPTER XXI

Jews dream of Palestine

If all the Jews had stayed in Europe, there would be very few of our people left in the world, because Hitler's Nazis would have killed them. But more than a hundred years ago, in 1848, there was a fight for freedom in Germany. The rulers put down the revolt and arrested the people's leaders. Many Jews as well as Germans who had fought for the people were forced to flee. They came to America.

Migrations to America

There had been small Jewish communities in America from its beginning, but now came a large wave of migration from Germany. And about fifty years later in Russia, the Czars, fearing a revolt of the people, turned the Russians against the Jews and let them take out their anger in pogroms. The Jews fled in great numbers. So there was a big wave of migration to America from Russia.

First the fathers came. They worked and saved enough money to send for their families. Jewish families grew, until there were almost as many Jews in this country as in the old country.

We know that our families came to America from Europe because they wanted to live freely. They came to escape the pogroms of Russia and Poland and other countries. We also know that many came because they had stepped out of the old way of life into the new Age of Enlightenment.

Some Jews went to Palestine

But not all the Jews who left the old country came to America. Some of them went to Palestine. Most of the immigrants chose America because America was a rich new land and a free land. And Palestine was a very poor country of stony hills and arid deserts. It was a small country and it was under the tyranny of the Turks. It had no freedom.

Yet, beginning about a hundred years ago, there were Jews who remembered the age-old dream of returning to Palestine. Though the great modern Zionist movement had not yet been organized, a few of the earliest pioneers went in small groups from Russia to Palestine.

What was it that started the Jews going back to Palestine, after all the centuries? In a way, it was the same movement of enlightenment and emancipation. Young people said, "Why shouldn't we Jews have a modern democracy? Why shouldn't we try to build up our old homeland into a modern country?"

Jews in many East European cities began to organize clubs and to train as farmers, so they could go and work on the land in Palestine. They began to study Hebrew and to talk Hebrew in their daily life instead of using it only for prayers.

Then something happened that quickly brought a great many more Jews into this movement. What happened was a terrible example of anti-Semitism, not in the backward or ignorant countries, but in one of the countries of emancipation. This happened before the "scientific" anti-Semitism of the Nazis in Germany.

The Dreyfus Case

The case happened in France. After the French Revolution, when Napoleon ruled France, he opened the ghettos and emancipated the Jews. But after Napoleon was defeated, many of the old enemies of the Jews began to spread anti-Semitic lies again. And the hatred of Jews came out in a very famous case called the Dreyfus Case.

Jews had been allowed to join the French Army, and some of them had even become officers. One of these was Captain Alfred Dreyfus. But there were officers in the army who hated Jews.

They were especially angry that a Jew should rise to be an officer.

One of the officers, Colonel Esterhazy, was acting as a spy against his own country, France. He was a traitor in the pay of the enemies of France, the Germans. When this spy was in danger of being caught, he and some friends forged some papers to make it look as if Captain Dreyfus had done the spying. Dreyfus was court-martialed and sent to Devil's Island.

But Dreyfus kept proclaiming his innocence. Many of the greatest French writers and lawyers became interested in the case, because they believed in fair

Captain Dreyfus is dishonored publicly

play and human rights. Some of these writers, like Emile Zola, showed that the case was not only a frame-up against Captain Dreyfus, but that it was a case of anti-Semitism.

And so the anti-Semitism became a very great question in France at that time. Those who hated the Jews were against Dreyfus, and those who believed in equality and justice for all people were on the side of Dreyfus in the famous case.

Theodor Herzl gets an idea

Finally the guilty parties were exposed and Dreyfus was freed. But during those years of excitement, people got to thinking about what it really means to be a Jew. One of the people who began to think about being a Jew, because of the Dreyfus case, was a famous newspaperman named Theodor Herzl. He was a foreign correspondent sent from Vienna to Paris to report about the Dreyfus case.

Theodor Herzl was a Jew who felt quite at ease in moving outside of Jewish circles. Most of his friends were authors and artists who did not pay great attention to whether a man was a Jew or not.

But when Theodor Herzl saw what happened to Captain Dreyfus, he asked himself how such a thing could happen in an enlightened country like France. How could a man be persecuted only because he was a Jew?

And Theodor Herzl got the idea that Jews would be respected only when they had a country of their own, like every other people. That country should

be their ancient land of Palestine. He wrote a book called *The Jewish State* in which he pleaded for this idea. He did not know that a number of Jews in Russia had already started to work on such a plan.

As Herzl was a brilliant writer and leader, his book quickly spread his thoughts to Jews all over the world. And soon they began to organize the Zionist movement. Theodor Herzl became the leader.

Zionist Congress convenes

A big meeting, the Zionist Congress, was held in Switzerland. To this meeting came representatives from Jewish groups in America, England, France, Russia and many other countries. There were men such as Max Nordau, Chaim Weizmann and Nahum Sokolow, who were to lead the movement later on. From then on,

the movement grew and grew, and more and more Jews went to Palestine to settle.

Not all Jews were in favor of the Zionist movement. Some Jews attacked Herzl and the Zionist idea, saying that Jews did not need to have a country of their own. They said that the Jewish homeland was in any land where Jews were allowed to live in freedom.

And from the other side, some highly orthodox Jews attacked the Zionists, for they believed it was not yet time for the Jews to go back to Palestine. They believed that the Messiah had to appear before the Jews could return to Zion.

Those who believed that Messiah was not a real person but a symbol thought that the Jewish people itself might rise to the mission of Messiah. And still others said that the movement was not a religious movement but a political

movement. In the Zionist Congress in Switzerland in 1897, the delegates agreed that "the aim of Zionism is to create for the Jewish People a home in Palestine secured by public law."

But who could make this public law? Herzl tried to convince the rulers of Europe to put their power behind the idea. He pleaded for his plan with the Kaiser of Germany, and with the king of Italy, and with the Pope, and with the prime minister of Great Britain. He even had an audience with the Sultan of Turkey, who was the ruler of Palestine. It was considered a great step—that kings and emperors would at least give an audience to a Jew speaking for his own people.

But Herzl died before he could see his dream come true. In his book, Herzl had said that he knew Palestine could not become a Jewish state in a few   145 years, but that he felt sure this would happen in fifty years. And fifty-one years later his dream came true. Israel declared itself an independent state and was admitted to the United Nations.

Fifty years of work and growth

In that fifty years, a great deal of work had been done. First in small numbers, then in large numbers, Jews had come to Palestine. There were nearly a million Jews in the land when the State of Israel was born. To make ready for the state, they had built towns and cities, schools and factories, theaters and shops.

Besides the Jews of Palestine who were working with their hands and brains to build up the land there were Jews all over the world to whom this task was one of the main tasks of their lives. They called themselves Zionists. A large number were members of the Zionist Organization; others did Zionist work, without being members. And still others did not think of themselves as Zionists, but still did a great deal to help build the Jewish settlement in Palestine.

Zionism becomes a way of life

For many Jews outside of Palestine, Zionism became almost a way of life in itself. We have seen how they raised money and attended meetings. They gave their support through petitions and speeches to the governments of the world to help establish a Jewish homeland. They worked in the Hadassah and in the Zionist Organization and for the Friends of the Hebrew University and for the Zionist Labor Federation and for many other groups.

Besides Theodor Herzl, there had been other Zionist leaders. One of them was Ahad Ha-Am whose name means "One of the People." He thought of Palestine as the spiritual and cultural center of all the Jews of the world. Another leader was A. D. Gordon who believed in uniting the Zionist ideal with the ideal of social justice. Jews returning to their own land would work with their own hands and share everything in a cooperative way. And this movement, as we shall see, led to important new ways of life for the Jews in Israel.

THINKING ABOUT WHAT YOU HAVE LEARNED

1. What did the first Zionist pioneers in Eastern Europe do to prepare themselves for life in Palestine?
2. How did the Dreyfus Case change Theodor Herzl's life?

QUESTIONS TO ASK YOUR PARENTS

1. Why did some Jews attack Herzl's idea about the need for a Jewish state? Are there Jews who still do so today?
2. What organizations in your community are most active today in helping the state of Israel?

CHAPTER XXII

Why Jews went back to Palestine

Sometimes people in different parts of the world are thinking the same thoughts without knowing about each other. Many great inventions have been thought of at the same time by people in different lands. The automobile, for instance, was invented in France and in America at almost the same time by men who didn't know about each other.

And so it was that the idea for the Jews to go back to Palestine was thought of by Theodor Herzl in Paris, when other Jews in Russia and in Poland were already starting farming settlements in the ancient homeland.

After Herzl became excited about his great idea, he began to study the history of the Jews. He learned that his idea had been in the hearts of the Jewish people ever since the time of the Patriarchs.

Zionism began with Abraham

Herzl went back to the stories of the Bible to understand Jewish history. And the Zionist pioneers who helped to fulfill Herzl's dream also went back to Jewish history for their ties with their homeland. They read again how Abraham was told to seek a land where he could worship God in freedom, and it seemed to them that this was true of their own lives—they were seeking a land where they, too, could live in freedom.

They read how Abraham was led to the land of Canaan, and how God promised it to him and his seed forever, and how Abraham loved the land and dwelt there and raised his family. The land of Canaan was the ancient name for Palestine, or Israel as it is called today.

But a famine sent the Jews away from Palestine. They went to Egypt to seek bread and there they became slaves. They couldn't get back to their beloved Palestine until Moses rose up to free them and Joshua led them homeward.

Kings and prophets made the land famous

Once more they were united with their beloved land, and they lived there and grew into a great nation. Their kings who reigned three thousand years ago— 147

In the time of Abraham, the Promised Land was pastoral

...rose to splendor under King Solomon

Saul and David and Solomon—are famous even today.

And they had other leaders, the prophets, who taught them that, to be worthy of the land they loved, they had to do good.

And some say it was because the Jews became sinful that they lost their beloved land. For they were conquered by the Babylonians. The Babylonians destroyed the first Temple in 586 B.C.E. on Mount Zion in Jerusalem, and took the Jewish people away into exile.

But the prophet Jeremiah told the people that their God could be worshipped even in exile, for their God asked of them only to do right. And the Jews studied their laws and tried to live by what was right all during the years they were in Babylon. And all that time, they tried to find a way to go back to their own land, to Palestine.

The Second Temple

At last a new king, Cyrus the Persian, allowed them to leave Babylonia. Many of the Jews left the homes they had built and the businesses they had started, and they went back to Jerusalem and rebuilt the Temple. This was called the Second Temple.

So once more the Jews were reunited with their beloved land. But after six hundred years the Romans came and destroyed the Second Temple in 70 C.E. They took many of the people as captives and slaves, and destroyed the farms. So most of the Jews had to seek to earn a living in other countries.

Poor as Palestine had become, there were scholars who clung to the schools where the Torah was studied. Jews

148

...declined to poverty under Arab domination

...returned to fertility in modern Israel

who had gone away to other lands to earn a living sent back money to Palestine to keep the schools going.

For nearly two thousand years there was no Jewish kingdom or nation in Palestine, and yet there were a few Jews. Also, from time to time Jews came from far places in the world to try to settle there again. Usually they came to study in the schools, or to pray at the Wailing Wall, the last piece of the Temple that was still standing.

The Golden Age and the Inquisition

After the first thousand years had passed, there came the Golden Age in Spain, when the Jewish community of Spain was prosperous. One of the greatest Jews of 12th century Spain was the poet Judah Halevi, who wrote love songs about Palestine, the land of his forefathers. Judah Halevi left Spain when he was an old man to travel to Jerusalem. But the country was infested with bandits, and it is said he was killed just as he arrived in his beloved land. Some of his poems were added to the books of prayers that we still use in our worship. They are prayers which express the hope of a return to the land of our fathers.

Bad times came with the Inquisition in Spain in 1492. Then the Jews were driven from one country to another in Europe, suffering from their enemies. They prayed for Messiah to come, to 149 lead them to their own land, and they believed that he would come when their troubles were greatest.

We have read about the false messiahs such as Sabbatai Zvi. And there were others. But the return to Palestine could not be accomplished as by a dream. Even Moses, you will remember, prepared the Jews for forty years in the wilderness before they were united and strong enough to enter the Promised Land.

The hope and the desire to return to the beloved land remained strong in the Jews from one century to another, from one generation to another. Then in modern times, they began to plan their return in a practical way.

Zionists studied the Bible for practical ideas

That was when the Zionist movement sprang up. And while it was a modern movement, it was linked to the old days through the entire history of the Jews. The modern Zionists studied the Bible not only as their history, but as their geography and as their book of agriculture. They studied it to learn how best to live in their old-new land.

They read how this had once been a land of milk and honey. And so the first pioneers brought with them modern breeds of cattle and they studied modern methods of bee-keeping. In Biblical days, much had been written of the vineyards of the Promised Land. And so the earliest of the modern settlers planted vineyards, and the wines of Rishon Le Zion and Zichron Yaacob were sent to Jews all over the world.

The new settlers remembered the copper mines of King Solomon, and searched for them in the deserts of the Negev. Now there are huge smelting and refining works, with the very latest machinery, operating where Solomon's workers once dug for copper.

While they tried to bring back the products of Biblical times, the new settlers sought for modern products, too, such as potash and oil. In fact, it was a line in the Bible, about the seepings of tar on the shores of the Dead Sea, that led them to seek for oil in Israel.

In their thinking also, the modern settlers reached back to the ideas of Biblical times, to the ideas of social justice of the great prophets. A new Jewish way of life was founded on the old.

THINKING ABOUT WHAT YOU HAVE LEARNED

1. Why is it said that Zionism began with Abraham?
2. What place do Judah Halevi and Sabbatai Zvi have in the history of the Zionist idea?

QUESTIONS TO ASK YOUR PARENTS

1. What is the significance of the "Wailing Wall" in Jewish history?
2. Discuss the similarities between the American pioneers and the Zionist pioneers.

CHAPTER XXIII

How Zionists started settlements in Palestine

People may talk about doing something, and dream about doing it, until everyone who knows them says, "They'll never really do it." But one day they surprise everyone, and do what they always said they would do.

A dream that did succeed

That is what happened with the Jews and Palestine. For years, for centuries, the Jews talked and wrote and dreamed about having their home in Palestine again. And many times they started out to win back Palestine, but didn't succeed. But as Theodor Herzl said, "If you will it, it is no dream."

As we have seen, the idea came to Jews in different parts of the world—Russia, Poland, Germany, Austria, France, England, America. Several of them wrote important books about the idea.

Rabbi Kalisher's book

Some of these books had been written long before Herzl's. In 1836, a famous rabbi wrote such a book. This was sixty years, or a whole lifetime, before Herzl. Rabbi Zvi Hirsh Kalisher wrote a pamphlet calling for a settlement of Jews in Palestine. He tried to interest wealthy Jews to give their money to start such colonies. He went to the Rothschilds and to Moses Montefiore, whom we have heard about. And he did get them to make a small start.

For in 1841, Sir Moses Montefiore bought an orange grove in Palestine. Today the orange-growing industry is the most important part of the agriculture in Israel.

Other Jews became interested in Rabbi Kalisher's ideas. But they found it strange that the small number of Jews who even then were living in Palestine did nothing to make the land bloom. The Jews who had been living there for generations were settled in the old cities of Jerusalem and Safed, and they did not know how to work the land. They used all their time for religious studies. They lived on charity from Jews in Europe.

An orange grove in Israel today

A Farming School at Mikveh Israel

But if there was to be a real Jewish community in Palestine again, there had to be Jewish farmers. Some of the leaders of the new movement said, "Why can't we begin with the people who already live in Palestine? Why shouldn't some of their children learn to grow food for the community, instead of depending on charity money?"

The first thing that was needed to bring about this healthful change in their way of life was a farming school.

And so in 1870, a school was started to train Jews to be farmers again, as they had been in Biblical days. This school was called Mikveh Israel, and it is still one of the most important and one of the best schools in Israel.

Moses Hess and Mordecai Noah

By the time this school was started, there had been other books and pamphlets published, urging Jews to revive their way of life in their own land. One of these was by Moses Hess. It was called "Rome and Jerusalem," and came out in 1862. Moses Hess tried to rally

falo, New York. But his plan did not succeed.

"Lovers of Zion"

In other countries, such plans began to have success. In Russia, clubs called "Lovers of Zion" were started in 1881, and their members, in small groups, began to move to Palestine. In the next twenty years, about 25,000 new settlers came to Palestine from Russia and Roumania.

It was in those twenty years that Zionism really got under way. Herzl's book was printed in 1895, fourteen years after the Lovers of Zion got started. And when he called for a World Zionist Congress, the largest group that came to the meeting in Switzerland were members from the Lovers of Zion clubs.

The First Aliyah

Those pioneers who went to Palestine in the earliest years came to be known as the "First Aliyah," or the first wave of immigrants. As we shall see, there were more such waves, each one of a very special kind.

But even though more Jews were settling in Palestine, the country did not belong to the Jewish people. At that time it was ruled by the Turks. It seemed that it would be very difficult for the Jews to secure Palestine as their own country, where they could have their own government.

This was the problem that worried the delegates who came to the World Zionist Congresses. By the time the fifth meeting was held, the problem had become very serious. There were new pogroms in Russia, and thousands of

Jews to go and live in Palestine, and to make it a center for the Jews of the world.

In the United States, there was a famous man named Mordecai Noah who wrote articles and made speeches urging the Jews to go back to Palestine. His idea was to prepare a large group of Jews in America, so that they would have the experience as a group to have their own government in Palestine. He even laid the foundation for such a colony, Ararat, on an island near Buf-

153

Jews longed only for a land where they could be their own rulers.

British Government offered Uganda

Some of the big nations studied this problem. They said that if the Jews couldn't have a government in Palestine, perhaps they would go somewhere else. Perhaps they would start in some other country.

The British government had control of a part of Africa called Uganda and they said they would be willing to help the Jews make a national home for themselves in Uganda.

Theodor Herzl thought that Uganda might be better than no place at all. Indeed, many strange places were suggested for the Jewish home. Among these places was the lower part of California, which is almost uninhabited.

But at the fifth Zionist Congress, the Lovers of Zion protested. Once and for all, they said, it should be decided that the Jews wanted no other place than Palestine for their national home. And so the Uganda idea, and all other ideas of that kind, were given up.

A children's nursery in a Kibbutz

154

Let each man work with his hands

About that time, a second big idea was growing among those who wanted to rebuild Palestine. The first idea had been simply to have a Jewish settlement in Palestine. But now many of the young men said, "What kind of life shall we lead there?"

Among these young people were idealists who believed that each man should do his own work with his own hands. They did not want to go to Palestine to become land-owners who employed Arabs to work for them. They said what A. D. Gordon had said: "Go up to the land, and let each man work with his hands to earn his bread." They were not ashamed to work with their own hands. They believed in the dignity of manual labor.

From 1904 to 1914, these were the leaders among the newcomers to Palestine. Their movement was known as the Second Aliyah. They started farm colonies in which all the members worked and shared. These colonies have become famous. They are called "kibbutzim." Their members had a strong pioneer spirit. They were called "halutzim."

The Second Aliyah came to a halt in 1914 because World War I broke out in Europe. By that time, the pioneers had raised the Jewish population of Palestine to 100,000. Many of the great leaders of Israel in later years had been members of this Second Aliyah. Among them was David ben Gurion who became the first Prime Minister of Israel.

From among the early settlers who belonged to the Lovers of Zion, and from the members of the Second Aliyah, came the main impulses for the new way of life in Israel. First was the feeling that this life had to be in the ancient Jewish homeland, and nowhere else. Second was the feeling that the new way of life had to be a balanced life. Jews should return to the soil as farmers. Jews should spread through every occupation, instead of being specialized in a few occupations, as they had been in European lands.

Kibbutzim as a way of life

They were particularly anxious to prove themselves as farmers. This was not only because Jews had for so long been separated from the soil, but because the first need for the nation was the production of food.

And to win back the neglected land, the Jewish pioneers found that it was best to work in groups. In this way they live more economically and work more effectively. And they could put into practice their social ideas of equality and cooperation.

Thus they organized themselves in groups called kibbutzim, groups of workers who shared their earnings and who lived cooperatively, with a common kitchen, and with nurseries for their children. And they worked their land in common and owned their livestock and farm machinery together. The kibbutz movement grew into a whole way of life in Israel, a way of life that was close to the ideal of the ancient Hebrew prophets who believed in justice and in equality.

The kibbutz movement was not the 155

only way of life in Israel. Other pioneers were private farmers, but with each family having an equal share of land, and dedicated to work its own soil. And there were factory workers and shopkeepers and clerks and professionals, too.

But the cooperative idea was a very strong part of Israel's way of life, so that even the bus lines were owned cooperatively by the bus drivers. In Israel it became easy to see how many forms the Jewish way of life could take, and still be as one whole because everything went back to the ideas of Judaism in the Bible.

THINKING ABOUT WHAT YOU HAVE LEARNED

1. Mikveh Israel means "Hope of Israel." Why would a farming school deserve such a name?
2. Aliyah, Kibbutz and Halutz are three important Hebrew words in the history of Zionism. Can you translate and explain them?

QUESTIONS TO ASK YOUR PARENTS

1. Why were so many of the early Zionists opposed to the offer of the British to settle Jews in Uganda?
2. What is the difference between the Kibbutz as a way of life and our own, especially in the care and raising of children?

An early settler in modern Palestine

CHAPTER XXIV

Hebrew is reborn

Just as the Jews had Sabbath clothes to wear on their day of worship, one might say also that they had a Sabbath language. It was their language of prayer, Hebrew. When the scholars spoke it, they felt close to Amos and Isaiah, and Moses at Mount Sinai.

Jews remembered Hebrew wherever they went

The Jews had kept the Hebrew language in their Torah and wherever they wandered in the world they carried it with them.

When different rulers had come into Palestine and conquered the Jews in ancient times, they had brought with them new languages—Aramaic and Greek and Syriac. The Jews had learned these languages, but they had not forgotten Hebrew.

And when the Jews were driven from their land, when they moved to different countries, they learned the language of those countries. In Babylonia, in Egypt, in Greece, in Rome, in Spain, they spoke and wrote the language of each place. But they prayed and studied in Hebrew.

Children were taught Hebrew as they studied the Bible and as they learned their prayers. Scholars of the Torah wrote their books in Hebrew. In Spain during the Golden Age, Jewish poets wrote their most beautiful works in Hebrew.

Most Jews were bilingual

Thus, most Jews knew at least two languages. Sometimes as we have seen with Yiddish, the two languages were mixed together. In Spain they mixed Hebrew words with Spanish, and a combination language called "Ladino" grew up.

In all these countries there were scholars and rabbis and writers who said that mixed languages were good enough for everyday use. But Hebrew must be kept pure.

Then came the time of the enlightenment and emancipation, when the Jews came out of the ghetto to mix in the world. You remember how in Germany, 157 led by Moses Mendelssohn, the Jews changed their old way of life. They translated the Bible into German so more Jews would learn to read German, and they read other books in German, too.

But some of the bright students in Russia had a different idea about the enlightenment. Instead of studying chemistry in another language, they decided to study it in Hebrew. They began to translate books of history and science and general world knowledge into the ancient Hebrew language.

Why did they want all this knowledge to be printed in Hebrew? It was part of their whole idea of rebuilding Jewish life. It was their way of bringing the new and the old together. It was part of the idea of Zionism and returning to live in Palestine.

The Jews asked themselves, "What language shall we speak when we go to live in our ancient land?" At that time, the Turks ruled Palestine. Should the Jews make Turkish their language? Arabs lived there. Should the new set-

A Hebrew newsstand in Tel Aviv

tlers speak only Arabic?

A battle of languages

This was not an easy question to settle, because there was already a mixup of languages in Palestine.

When the French Jews gave money for a farming school in Palestine, the teaching was in French. When German Jews gave money for a technical school in Haifa, the teaching was in German. Soon there were other schools using English. Clearly, one language had to become the main language. There was quite a battle to see which language would win.

The Zionist idealists believed that the main language should be Hebrew, even if the other languages had a head start. Of course there were some disadvantages in using Hebrew. While it was not a dead language, it was a historical language. It was a language that was not used every day.

There were no Hebrew newspapers in those days, and there were no Hebrew words for many modern things, like railways, telegraphy, steam engines, or even for tobacco and for different foods that had not been known in Biblical days.

And there were pious Jews who believed that Hebrew was strictly a holy language that should not be spoiled by everyday use.

Eliezer ben Yehuda

Among the idealists who wanted to use Hebrew in daily life was a young Russian Jew named Eliezer Perlman. He came to Palestine at the time of the Second Aliyah, with settlers who spoke Yiddish and Russian. There he changed his name to Eliezer ben Yehuda.

In their new way of life the new settlers had many things to learn. They had to learn to work on the land and to live in the Palestinian climate. They had to learn how to deal with the Turks and the Arabs. On top of all this, to learn to use Hebrew as their everyday language seemed too much to ask.

But Eliezer ben Yehuda was a man with a cause. First of all, he made a rule in his own home that no word but Hebrew should be spoken. When his first child was born he forbade that any word but Hebrew should come to the baby's ears. He and his wife began to teach the shopkeepers to transact business only in Hebrew. And when words were missing for some of the modern things in the stores, Eliezer ben Yehuda supplied the new words.

How new words were made

He did not exactly make them up. In fact, he tried his best not to bring in words from other languages as had been done with Yiddish. Instead, he sought for the roots of old Hebrew words which could be put together to become names for the new things. For example, there was no Hebrew word for newspaper. Eliezer ben Yehuda took the Hebrew word *et* which means "time," and said that the word for newspaper would be *iton* or "times."

Eliezer ben Yehuda was so fanatical about using Hebrew that he even refused an inheritance that came to him from Russia, because he would have had to sign for it in his old name, Perlman. *159*

THING	HEBREW	NAME	OLD GREEK	NAME	ROMAN
OX	א	ALEPH	Α	ALPHA	A
HOUSE	ב	BETH	Β	BETA	B
CAMEL	ג	GIMEL	Γ	GAMMA	C
DOOR	ד	DALETH	Δ	DELTA	D
WINDOW	ה	HE	Ε	EPSILON	E
WEAPON	ז	ZAYIN	Ι	ZETA	Z
FENCE	ח	CHETH	⊟	ETA	H
HAND	י	YOD	)	IOTA	I
GOAD	ל	LAMED	∠	LAMBDA	L
WATER	מ	MEM	Μ	MU	M

The letters of our alphabet originally were pictures of *things*. Ancient Hebrew letters were similar to those of neighboring peoples. Sometimes letters were simply turned on their sides, or strokes would be added. Together they helped give us the alphabet we use today, which is based directly on the Roman alphabet. Even the names given the letters by the Hebrews, Greeks and Romans were similar.

He began to prepare a dictionary of new Hebrew words. He published a weekly "iton" in Hebrew. He started a great argument about using only Hebrew in the schools. And finally, after calling a strike in the technical school in Haifa, he got the teaching changed from German to Hebrew.

Bialik—Hebrew poet and teacher

Of course Eliezer ben Yehuda was not alone in his ideas. Along with him were such great men as the poet Chaim Nachman Bialik, who also had once been a yeshiva student in Russia. Bialik could write in both Yiddish and Hebrew, but he became a Hebrew teacher and wrote his great poetry in Hebrew, the language of the Bible and of modern Palestine.

Even when he was world famous, Bialik felt that the most important work he could do was to educate children. He wrote for them in Hebrew so they could grow up with their own language.

By the time Eliezer ben Yehuda and Bialik and their many helpers had accomplished their work, there were several daily Hebrew newspapers and many magazines in Hebrew. Hebrew was the language of the land.

Three official languages

After the First World War, Palestine was taken away from the Turks. In those days, before there was a United Nations, there was the League of Nations. The League put England in charge of Palestine until the people of the country could have their own government. When the English took charge, they made Hebrew, Arabic and English the three official languages of Palestine. All street signs were printed in three languages, one above the other, and all official notices were posted up in those languages. And all the schools taught all three languages.

Thirty years later, when the British left, and Israel declared itself a free nation, of course there was no longer any question about Hebrew. By then, Hebrew was the natural as well as the official language of the country, because it was the language spoken from birth of the children of Eliezer ben Yehuda and the children of all the other Jews who had come to rebuild the land. They even had slang in Hebrew.

One of history's miracles

There is perhaps no other example in all history of a language coming back to life. To the outside world, the rebirth of Hebrew is one of the great miracles of history.

Not only has Hebrew become a living language in Israel, where it is the language of daily life, but it has again become a living language all over the world.

Eliezer ben Yehuda would never have dreamed of this!

THINKING ABOUT WHAT YOU HAVE LEARNED

1. What kept Hebrew alive for 2000 years after the Jews were exiled from Palestine?
2. What did Eliezer ben Yehudah do to make Hebrew the official language of Palestine?

QUESTIONS TO ASK YOUR PARENTS

1. Latin and Greek are taught in some of our schools. How does the use of Hebrew differ from the use of Latin and Greek in the world today?
2. What is being done in your community to give Jewish children and adults an opportunity to learn Hebrew as a living language?

CHAPTER XXV

The State of Israel is born

You may wonder exactly how a people can get a country of their own. This happens in different ways. Far back in history there were not so many settled countries. There were wandering tribes. And the tribes would wander through wastelands and sometimes find a good place and settle down to raise crops and sheep and cattle. This would become their land, their country.

Land may be bought or conquered

Sometimes wandering people would come into a land where others already lived, and they would conquer the people who were there. Sometimes, as in the case of America, civilized people would come to a land that was inhabited by only a small number of people who had a more primitive civilization. The new people would buy part of the land not being used by the tribes, and settle on it. Sometimes also they would conquer the tribes because they had better weapons and believed they could make better use of the land.

We have seen that after the Jews were driven from Palestine, the country was conquered again and again by different peoples, until in modern times the Turks were the rulers. As you know, everyone wanted Palestine because of its strategic location. But nobody cared much for the land itself because it was a weak and poor land. The trees had been cut down and burned. The rains had been allowed to wash the soil from the mountains so that only rocks remained.

Jews start to buy land in Palestine

When Herzl started the Zionist organization, he thought that since Palestine had become such a poor country and since not very many people lived there, the Jews might even be able to buy the entire land from the Sultan of Turkey. But this did not work out.

Then the Zionists started the Jewish National Fund, to buy large sections of land in Palestine. In this way, the Jewish people would come to own large areas. Much of the land in Palestine was owned by "effendi," the landlords who did not even live there and did not raise crops. They let the land go to waste. Some of these effendi sold tracts of land to the Jews. The Jewish settlers drained the swamps and irrigated the deserts and made the land useful again. That is how the first Jewish colonies in Palestine were started.

But how could the Jews ever hope to become their own rulers in Palestine? Some thought they could conquer the land by force from the Turks. Others thought it might come about through a treaty, after many thousands of Jews had moved into Palestine and become the majority.

Jews in the British army

But in the modern world, the fate of every country and of every people is not always in its own hands. It sometimes depends on what is happening in the rest of the world. In 1914, there was a great upheaval among the nations, the First World War. It lasted four years. On one side were Russia, England, France, America and several other countries. They were called the Allies. On the other side were mainly the Germans, Austrians and Serbians. The Turks joined that side.

The war was fought on many battlefields. One was Palestine. For since the Turks ruled Palestine, the Allies attacked there. A British army invaded the land to weaken the Turks and the Germans.

Irrigation made the land bloom again

163

In the British army was a special brigade of Jews. Most of them had come to live in Palestine during the Second Aliyah. They saw their chance to get rid of Turkish rule and volunteered to fight on the Allied side. And with them were Jewish volunteers from many countries—from England, France, Russia and America.

Their special brigade was part of the British army led by General Allenby, and it was this army that won Palestine from the Turkish rulers.

Weizmann's invention made the British grateful

There was another way in which the Zionists helped the Allies to win the First World War. One of the leading Zionists of the world, Dr. Chaim Weizmann, was also a great chemist. He had been born in a small Russian town, but had been led by the movement of enlightenment to study chemistry, and after that he had come to England to work at Manchester University.

During the war he invented a new way to make an explosive which proved of great help to the Allies. The English

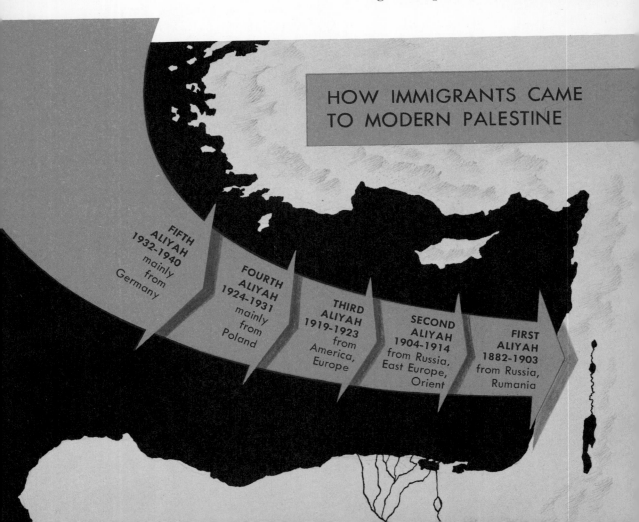

HOW IMMIGRANTS CAME TO MODERN PALESTINE

FIFTH ALIYAH 1932-1940 mainly from Germany

FOURTH ALIYAH 1924-1931 mainly from Poland

THIRD ALIYAH 1919-1923 from America, Europe

SECOND ALIYAH 1904-1914 from Russia, East Europe, Orient

FIRST ALIYAH 1882-1903 from Russia, Rumania

felt grateful to Dr. Weizmann for this invention. And so they were ready to listen when he asked them to help the Zionist cause.

You may wonder why England, a country far away from Palestine, had so much to do with the fate of that land. But the English nation is an Empire, which means it is a league of different countries scattered all over the world. Thus, England is one of the great powers in the world.

The Balfour Declaration

When Palestine was won from the Turkish rulers, there was no government in Palestine except the British army. The Jews claimed they had a right to set up a government. But all around Palestine were countries inhabited by Arabs. And some of these Arabs wanted to rule Palestine, too.

The British listened to all the claims. They were friendly to Jewish leaders but also to the Arab chieftains. Who should get Palestine after the war?

Before the war was over, the British gave an answer to this question. It was given by the man in charge of foreign affairs in their government, Lord Balfour. In 1917 he wrote the famous Balfour Declaration which stated that the government of England viewed "with favor the establishment in Palestine of a National home for the Jewish people."

Lord Balfour sent this statement to the most important English Jew, Lord Rothschild, as the Rothschild family had helped to start some of the first Zionist settlements. The whole world understood this declaration to mean that at last the Jews were to have their homeland. In the United States, President Wilson gave the blessing of our government and of the American people to this idea.

After the declaration was made, the League of Nations decided that the English should have charge of Palestine until the country was able to run its own government. England was given a mandate to govern Palestine for a number of years, and meanwhile to help it to become the Jewish national home.

A third and a fourth Aliyah

After the war, came the third great wave of immigrants to Palestine. This was the Third Aliyah, for with the Balfour Declaration, thousands of Jews felt sure that the homeland was really reborn. Many new colonies were established. Cities grew, especially Tel Aviv and Haifa. The Hebrew University was started in Jerusalem. Hospitals and schools were built throughout the land. Factories sprang up. Jews all over the world gave large sums of money to the Jewish National Fund to buy sections of land for Jewish farmers.

Arabs sold land to the Jews and became rich. But some Arabs caused trouble. Some attacked Jewish settlements. The Jews formed groups of watchmen to defend the settlements. Later on this self-defense organization came to be called the Haganah.

Jewish settlements grew. When Hitler became the ruler of Germany and started to persecute Jews, tens of thousands of German Jews moved to Palestine. They were another wave of immi-

Israel's war for independence

grants, the Fifth Aliyah.

And then came another World War.

The gates are closed

You have read how during World War II millions of Jews were killed in Europe. At the end of the war, those who remained alive no longer wanted to live in the lands where their families had died. Most of them wanted to live in the Jewish homeland.

The gates to the homeland were still closed. But hundreds of thousands of Jews started toward Palestine, and all over the world a great clamor was raised that the Jews ought to be allowed to enter their homeland. But the British did not agree.

So fighting broke out in Palestine between the Jews and the British Mandate government who would not allow more Jews to enter. And the Arabs continued their attacks against the Jews.

Israel becomes a state

At last the United Nations decided the question, by voting. More than two thirds of the members of the United Nations voted to have Palestine divided into two areas, Jewish and Arab. And they decided that a Jewish state should be set up in the Jewish area.

Instead of agreeing, the Arabs started a war against the Jews of Palestine. The British declared their mandate was at an end, and left the country. Then on

May 14, 1948, the Jews declared that the State of Israel was born, and they formed their own government for the first time in nineteen hundred years. They beat off the attacks of the Arabs, and the State of Israel was established.

Israel was admitted to membership in the United Nations. The flag of Israel was raised amongst the flags of all the other nations. The Jewish people had proved the endurance of their beliefs, and the vitality of their way of life.

THINKING ABOUT WHAT YOU HAVE LEARNED

1. How are the names of Balfour and Weizmann linked in the history of modern Israel?
2. In what year did Israel become an independent state? What part did the UN have in this event?

QUESTIONS TO ASK YOUR PARENTS

1. How did the Jews obtain land in Palestine as compared to the ways in which other modern nations obtained their land?
2. What problems do the Israelis face because many Arabs fled from their homes during the Arab-Israeli war?

CHAPTER XXVI

New Ways of Life in Israel

Now that Israel is again a nation, you may wonder what it is like to live there. Is it like it was nineteen hundred years ago? Do the Jews tend sheep, and travel up to the Temple in Jerusalem for the holidays? Or is it like Jewish life today in any other country, for example, your own?

Some things remain, others change

You know that your own life keeps changing all the time as you grow older, and yet some things in it are the same. Some things that you do with your family have been the same since you were very small and could first notice and remember.

So it is with the Jewish people. Some things, like the belief in One God and in doing right, are the same as they were in the time of Moses and the prophets. And other things are changing.

For instance, the last time there was a Jewish government in Israel, it was a government of a king. Today it is a democracy. While there are still shepherds on the hills, there are also tractors in the fields. There is no Temple in Jerusalem, but there are many synagogues, and there is a knesseth, or congress.

Jews bring many ways of life to Israel

And the Jews of Israel have many of the problems of the early settlers of America. To America, there came people from all parts of the world, to form one nation and one government. The same thing is happening in Israel.

For instance, there are Jews who come from the kingdom of Yemen, far down in Arabia. They had been living as if in Bible times for centuries. These Jews were brought to Israel in big American planes. This was called Operation Magic Carpet. You can see pictures of the Yemenites, how dark they are, and what strange clothes they wear.

But before the Jews from Arab lands started to come to Israel in great numbers, there were the Jews who came from Europe. Jews who had managed to survive in the concentration camps, and others who had escaped the Nazis, came to Israel. They were not used to the way of life of the Zionist pioneers and they had to be helped and taught.

So all these groups of Jews from different countries and with different customs are making the new Israel, just as the pioneers and immigrants from different lands made America. And in the new Israel, a new Jewish way of life is coming into being. The Israelis are being brought together not only by living in the same place. They are for the first time all using the same language, Hebrew. And in the schools their children are all studying together.

Problems of religious practice

But there are still many great problems. The biggest problems have to do with religious practices. Here in America, the Jews have different religious practices, some orthodox, some conservative and some reform. In Israel, the problem is harder.

The orthodox Jews in Israel believe that because Israel is the Holy Land, it should be as in the old days, a government that is linked up with religion. They believe that the laws should force people to obey all the Sabbath rules, and that the laws should stand behind the rules of Kashruth.

Yet many of the pioneer Zionist lead-

Operation Magic Carpet

169

ers were emancipated Jews. They believe that even in Israel people should be free to worship as they choose, just as in other countries. Or not to worship at all.

Until recent years, the orthodox synagogues were the only ones in Israel. And many pioneers felt they did not need synagogues at all. They felt that by living in Israel they were keeping alive the Jewish ideas that were kept alive in other lands by the synagogues.

New ways of celebrating holidays

Thus the non-observant pioneers celebrated the holidays as national holidays with customs of their own. They observed the Sabbath as a day of rest, but few of them went to a worship service.

Many settlements did have an "Oneg Shabbat," a pleasant gathering, with music and perhaps a lecture or a discussion or a reading of poetry. This type of Sabbath celebration was started by the great Hebrew poet, Bialik, and is now very popular not only in Israel but in Jewish communities in America and other lands.

On Purim the Israeli pioneers had street processions and a carnival, and on Tu B'shvat they planted forests on the rocky hills. On Passover, they changed the seder service to include stories of their escape into Israel. You can see that they were adding new ways to the traditional holiday celebrations.

And this new Jewish way of life is bringing some changes into our Jewish ways here in America. For example, besides adopting Oneg Shabbat, we like to dance Israeli dances and we like to sing Israeli songs.

Another important link to the Israeli way of life is our study of Hebrew. More and more of us are studying Hebrew not only in our temples and community centers, but in high schools and colleges. For Hebrew is a living language again.

The ways of life flow together

And if we want to think how all ways of life flow together, we may remember the teaching of the Hassidim, and how they felt that the greatest worship was through joy, and that the most wonderful prayer could be a song without words.

This is not so far from the spirit of the Israeli pioneers. In the fields of Israel they express some of the same feelings the Hassidim expressed in their synagogues.

Because of our interest in Israel, we feel that all the parts of our history have come together. We get a thrill when we read of a new settlement springing up in the same spot and with the same name as a town of Biblical times.

And as in Temple days, when many Jews lived in Palestine and many Jews lived in Babylonia and there was much travel between the two communities, so today there is a great deal of travel between America and Israel.

Israeli airplanes carry people back and forth to both countries. Israeli ships carry students and tourists from other countries to and from Israel.

But you must not think that day to day living in Israel is so different from ours. The Israelis go to the movies, read books in English and go to modern schools. They drink sodas, eat ice cream and dress much as we do, except that the men wear shorts in hot weather. And they usually leave off neckties.

All around Israel are Arab countries, and most Arabs have a different way of life. Many live in huts and tents, and have few machines to help them in their work. As they look at their neighbors in Israel, the Arab people see that even in their part of the world they can have a modern life, with good schools for their children, and machinery on their farms.

So through the example of Israel, the Arabs are being helped forward. The whole world looks on the Israeli way of life as bringing modern ideas, health and progress to a part of the world that has been backward and poor.

THINKING ABOUT WHAT YOU HAVE LEARNED

1. How did the Jews come from Yemen to Israel and what was this event called?
2. What new ways of observing Jewish holidays have developed in Israel?

QUESTIONS TO ASK YOUR PARENTS

1. Are there Orthodox, Conservative and Reform Jews in Israel, or is there an official religion?
2. Will Israel help to bring peace and prosperity to the Arab lands?

UNIT SIX

"... and they shall beat t.

The Jewish
Way of Life
today and
tomorrow

ords into plowshares, and their spears into pruning hooks . . . and the wolf the lamb shall lie down together."

CHAPTER XXVII

Are different Ways so different?

We have been studying a way of life. What makes people live one way instead of another?

Sometimes it is the climate of the place in which they live. This will influence what they eat and how they dress, whether they stay indoors very much or do things outdoors. It will determine whether they have much spare time to play and think, or whether they must work hard all the time to get a living from bad soil. It will affect their thoughts—whether they fear nature and imagine frightful gods, or whether they love the world and believe in goodness.

Then, as a civilization grows, a way of life is found in how the people live with each other, whether in small groups or in large groups, in families or in tribes. A way of life is seen in how they rule themselves, by elders or by kings or by priests, or as a group in which each man has an equal voice.

Judaism is our way of life

We have seen how the Jewish way of life grew through the wisdom of the patriarchs who understood that there was One God and who believed that God wanted people to do right toward one another. This is the way that is called Judaism. And during the centuries of life of the Jewish people, their religion, Judaism, was the main guide in their way of life.

It was stronger than kings, it was stronger than conquerors. It held them together no matter in what country they lived. For it was a collection of laws and of customs and of history, and it was a religion which they believed Moses brought to them from God.

Other religions guide other ways of life

Just as Judaism was a religion that gave our people its way of life, so there are other religions that have guided the ways of life of other people. Most of the great religions have an idea of One God, most of the great religions have stories about the first man who understood their message of God. Each of the great religions has its own ceremonies and festivals. Each of the great religions has answers about how the world was created, about how men should deal with each other, about why men have to work for their living and about what happens to people when they die.

The believers in each religion feel that its founders were given the true faith from God. The believers in some religions feel that other people should share their beliefs. And they have used various ways to make this happen.

Sometimes they used force, and people who refused to change their own religion were put to death.

Sometimes they used arguments, and believers in one religion tried to show others that their religion was the best.

A third way is by example. People who believe in this way try to live as their religion teaches them, and hope that others will see that their way of life is good and will want to live in the same way.

Judaism believes in setting a good example

Judaism has believed in this third way. Judaism has not used force to make people believe as the Jews believe. And Jews have not tried to convince other people by arguments to become Jews. They have only hoped that other people would adopt the ideas of God's justice that are the center of the Jewish faith.

The Jewish way is by example

As the center of the center, the Ten Commandments have indeed been adopted by people of other great faiths. While the Ten Commandments were given to the Jews on Mount Sinai, they are looked upon as laws for all men. Since that time, Christians and Muslims have made these Commandments a part of their religions.

Other teachings and customs of the Jews have also been accepted by believers in different religions. The Muslims gather together for prayer without the need of a priestly leader, just as a group of ten Jews may gather together for worship without a rabbi or official leader.

The story of the three rings

So you see that ways of life may go down different roads, but they all lead to God. Perhaps you can see this idea in a story that is told about three rings.

There was a good man who had three sons. As he grew old, and knew that one day he must die, he thought about his most valuable worldly possession, which was a ring with precious stones. He wondered to which son he should leave this ring. It was a very difficult decision to make, for he loved all his sons.

Then he thought of a way. He had two rings made which looked exactly like the real one. He called his sons together and gave each one of them a ring. He told them that the son who would live the most righteous life would one day discover that he had the true ring.

In this way, the father hoped that each of his three sons would try to live as a good man, a righteous man. And if all three sons lived righteously, it would be the same as if each one had been given the true ring worn by the father.

There is no puzzle to this story. It only tells us that all ways of life can be ways of good life, if men will want to make them so.

THINKING ABOUT WHAT YOU HAVE LEARNED

1. How have believers in each religion tried to convince others that their way is the "true way"?
2. How does the parable of "The Three Rings" show a Jewish point of view toward life?

QUESTIONS TO ASK YOUR PARENTS

1. How have so many different "ways of life" developed throughout the world?
2. Would it be better if all people had one religion?

CHAPTER XXVIII

What religions want for us

Have you ever heard the song about raisins and almonds? It is a Yiddish cradle song, a favorite song that mothers used to sing as they rocked their babies to sleep.

When Messiah comes,
Oh when Messiah comes,
All of us will feast on
Raisins and almond nuts,
When Messiah comes . . .

It tells of all the other wonderful things that will happen when Messiah comes. It is like an idea of a heaven.

And have you ever heard another song, a Negro spiritual, called "All God's Chillun Got Shoes"?

Heav'n, Heav'n,
Gonna walk all over God's heav'n . . .

For to the poor Negro children in the days of slavery, just to have a pair of shoes on their feet meant heaven.

A dream of Heaven on Earth

So each people expresses in its religion its wishes—its simple wishes and its grand wishes. Every religious group has a dream of a world when people will have what they most want. They may sing of almonds and raisins or of having shoes, but we all know what they want—they want peace and plenty.

Sometimes, having all this is called Heaven or the kingdom of God on earth.

Many legends are told about the peace that would come at the "end of days" when the world had become perfect. There would be peace not only among men, but among animals. The great prophet Isaiah spoke of the time when "the wolf and the lamb will lie down together."

So we see that in this religious feeling there is a wish for friendship among all living creatures, for peace. It is a wish and a dream in the hearts of men, and through their religions they try to bring themselves closer to behaving in a way that will make that dream come true.

The Ten Commandments are a beginning

First, the Ten Commandments teach people how to live at peace with each other. Then the Torah teaches man to

177

settle disputes, and it tells us that the stranger, the poor and the homeless shall also have their share of the good things of life.

This is our goal. All through history men have been trying to make themselves better, to control their angry impulses, so that they may reach that goal. The Jews reminded themselves of it with the word they used whenever people met. They said "Shalom," "Peace," as they met and again as they parted.

Other religions shared this ideal. The Christians in their prayer service repeat the same thoughts that are found again and again in Jewish prayerbooks. "Peace on earth . . ." belongs to all religions.

You may wonder why, if everyone believes in these ideals, we still have strife and wars. If religions say that all men are brothers, why do they hurt each other?

We must master envy and fear

Our wise, ancient stories can help us understand that, too, for our very oldest stories tell us of Cain and Abel, and how one brother killed another out of envy. We see that man is not perfect as God is perfect. We see that man needs codes by which to live. We see that man needs goals to strive for.

Religion gives us our code and our goals. It teaches us to live as good men.

Peace is the goal of mankind, and slowly we have been working toward it. Through the United Nations, the member nations hope to be able to talk out their fears and their envies, so that peace may come to the whole world.

THINKING ABOUT WHAT YOU HAVE LEARNED

1. If you were asked to write additional verses to the song. "When Messiah Comes . . ." what would you write about things to eat, to wear, to play, etc?
2. Why is the Biblical verse about the "wolf and the lamb" an appropriate symbol of a world at peace?

QUESTIONS TO ASK YOUR PARENTS

1. If we follow the Ten Commandments, will we achieve the goals of religion?
2. Why do the differences among religions often cause conflicts when their goals are the same?

CHAPTER XXIX

Much we do not know

Every way of life that has grown from a religion, as Judaism has grown, really has the same goal. Because we speak of the "way" we know that it is a path or a road, and every path leads somewhere. It is true that we may sometimes take a wandering path, in life as in the world, simply for the pleasure of wandering. Or we may start on a path that wanders and twists and we may become worried and even frightened because we don't know where it leads, or whether it leads to the place we want to reach.

The idea of heaven

What is that place? In Judaism, as in most religions, the goal is thought by some people to be heaven. We have many legends that tell us about the life to come, and about the joys of heaven. We also have stories that tell of our hope for a good life "when Messiah comes."

And just as we have said that Messiah is within ourselves, we feel, too, that the idea of heaven can grow within ourselves through our deeds.

The way of life that we speak of is a path of deeds, of behavior in life. At each step we have to decide how to behave, whether to say yes or no to a friend who wants to get into mischief, whether to join a group taunting a new boy in school or whether to make friends with that boy. We have to decide whether to do our studies well or whether to skim through them and pick up the answers in such a way that it will be hard to tell if we really studied. We have to decide such things all our lives, even as adults.

Our way of life and the ideas that we have been taught by our people help us at each step to make these decisions. But the decisions on how to behave are not always simple. Good and evil, right and wrong, are not always clear. That is why people have pondered about it since the beginning of civilization. That is why hundreds of scholars worked for hundreds of years to make up the Talmud and why, to this day, other rabbis and scholars keep on explaining what is meant.

179

The Torah guides us in the atomic age

The more science discovers, the greater the mystery

For as people discover new things in science, they wonder how the old rules apply. We live in the age of scientific discovery. Each day we have new knowledge. For the first time in the history of mankind we have reached into outer space. We have even gone beyond the moon.

If we learn all these things, will we come too close to God? The best of our scientists tell us that the more they learn, the more they are awed by the beauty and the mystery of the universe, and the more they feel the presence of God.

Some people think that if we keep on making discoveries, we will discover the secret laws of the universe, and that everything will prove to be only a huge, complicated machine.

Some people say that as we discover the mechanical laws of nature, we will find out that everything can be mechanical, and that therefore there is no such thing as right or wrong, good or evil. They even say that there is no moral law because in our lives we all find moral laws disproven.

Why don't the evil always suffer?

They tell us that everybody in his life has seen times when evil is rewarded and goodness leads to suffering. And this cannot be denied. We all see it happening. We all know people who behave badly and don't seem to suffer for it. Indeed, they seem to be rewarded.

There are people who cheat in business and yet get rich and enjoy themselves. There are people who make slaves of others and yet are honored and respected.

There are people who start wars, only to gain more power for themselves, and yet nothing bad seems to happen to them. In the end, it is true, a dictator like Hitler was defeated and he killed himself, but only after he had brought great evil on the earth.

What is the answer? We don't know the final answer any more than we know the name or the face of God. That is why Abraham was so inspired, so wise. He understood that man was far, far from knowing such answers and that man might never know them completely unless God willed him to.

But he understood also that man had to search for God's way and he imparted this understanding to us. All of our modern science—with its microscopes and telescopes and radar and space tracers and rockets and uranium—all this science is still the same search for God's way that was going on thousands of years ago in the desert when our ancestors raised their eyes to the heavens and noticed and watched the paths of the planets and the stars.

And in this search we are guided not only by our minds, but by a great feeling. We are guided by a feeling of joy that comes when we do what we feel is right. It is the best feeling a man can have.

And how are we to choose, how are we to know what is right or wrong in any problem that comes before us in life?

We cannot always know for sure. But we can be helped by the guideposts in our way of life, by the knowledge that has come from our ancestors, who have been through the same or similar problems.

The story of Job

They, too, faced the deepest problem of all, the problem of the evil that sometimes seems to come, and sometimes really does come, even after a man has done good deeds. They faced it, and they told a deep story about this problem. The story is in the Bible. It is called the Book of Job.

Job was a good man. He was righteous and fair, and he worked hard and he loved God. He avoided evil. He wanted to be perfect.

And he was a man in good circumstances. The story tells us that he had seven thousand sheep and three thousand camels and five hundred yoke of oxen and five hundred donkeys and a very large household, and that he was the greatest man in the East.

Job had seven sons and three daughters. And when the holidays came, he sacrificed to the Lord, as Abraham had done. He offered burnt offerings not only for himself, but for his sons too, so that if they had sinned they might be forgiven.

Then Satan came to the Lord and said, "Give him to me to test out." He said that if troubles came to Job, if Job was rewarded with evil times for his good deeds, he would forget his love of

God and curse the Almighty. The Lord agreed to the test.

Enemies came and took away Job's oxen and his donkeys. Lightning came and destroyed his flocks of sheep. A whirlwind came when Job's sons and daughters were feasting together in the house of the eldest, and his children all died.

But Job said, "Naked was I born, and naked will I die. The Lord gave, and the Lord hath taken away. Blessed be the name of the Lord."

Job does not lose faith in God

But Satan was not satisfied with this test. He made Job suffer even more. His whole body was stricken and he was covered with boils and sores. Then Job became bitter. He cursed the day he was born. He said he wished he never had been born.

Yet he did not lose his faith. Job tried to understand what had happened to him. He talked about it to his friends.

They told him not to become lost in his bitterness, but to see the wonders of the universe and to remember the greatness of God. "What use is anger?" they asked. "Wrath kills the foolish man, and envy slays the silly one." They reminded Job that man lives just a little while, but that God is eternal; and the troubles of one man may be meaningful in the eternal scheme of things. And indeed we know that the troubles of Job were meaningful, for the story of how he was tested has come down through the ages to help us.

They talked and talked, for it helps people to talk about their troubles. Job said he was weary of life. He said, "I cry out of my wrong, but I am not

A mighty wind destroys Job's house

heard." He said all the things that we say when we are hurt and we feel that we have been unfairly treated.

"Wherefore do the wicked live?" he asked, "and even become mighty in power? They drink, and feast without end, and do every kind of wrong to people. They violently take away the flocks of others, and yet nothing happens to them!"

When his friends spoke to him of the vastness, the greatness of the Lord, when they reminded him that God does strike the wicked, he still was not satisfied.

Voice of God out of a whirlwind

They reminded him of the wonders of the universe, of thunder, rain, and snow, of the heat of the sun. They asked Job to look at the sky, and then to compare the smallness of man to the greatness of God. "Hast thou with him spread out the sky, which is strong, and as a molten looking glass?"

After all his friends had spoken, the voice of God came to Job. The Lord answered Job out of a whirlwind.

And the Lord asked,

"Where wast thou when I laid down the foundations of the earth? Hast thou commanded the morning since thy days began, and caused the dayspring to know its place? Hast thou cleft a channel for the waterflood?

Hast thou given the horse strength?

Hast thou clothed his neck with thunder?"

And the Lord asked Job, "Shall a man try to teach God? Shall he that contendeth with the Almighty instruct him? Let the man who complains against God answer all the questions of the universe."

Learning to face troubles

Then Job at last became humble. He said, "I am vile." And the Lord said, "Gird up thy loins like a man." For Job had to learn to face his troubles. God asked of man that he face evil, face misfortune and prove himself the greater.

This Job did. And the story tells us that the Lord blessed the later days of Job more than the beginning. He had fourteen thousand sheep and six thousand camels and a thousand yoke of oxen and a thousand donkeys, and again he had seven sons and three daughters. And there were no women to be found as fair as the daughters of Job.

What does this story tell us? It tells us that Job withstood his test by learning not to be too proud. But it cannot tell us the final answer to why evil sometimes comes even if we are good.

Perhaps it is to test all of us as Job was tested. Perhaps it is to teach us that good actions should not be done for a reward, but for themselves. But also it is to show us that Judaism endlessly studies this most profound of human problems and that we, like our fathers and our forefathers, must not grow too proud of our success and our knowledge. It reminds us of the great saying of the prophet Micah, that can be a rule of life, "To do justly, to love mercy, and to walk humbly with thy God." That is the best man can do.

The vastness of the unknown

To walk humbly means to recognize that we don't know everything. We recognize this when we turn to the wisdom of our people for guidance in our way of life. Our traditional Jewish laws teach us not only of the things that are known, but they remind us of the vastness of the unknown. Our ceremonies, our days of prayer, our days of fasting, our days of remembrance of slavery in the past, our days of thankfulness for the fruits of the earth—all these landmarks in our way of life help us to express our feelings about life and about God.

These expressions of feeling are necessary to us, not only to show those around us that we think and search with them, not only to give us the feeling of belonging, but to satisfy our own selves. We have an inner need to express our feelings. It was this same need that made Abraham put stones together for an altar to worship the One God. It was this same need that made David sing to the Lord on his harp. It was this same need that gave birth to the services in our synagogue.

It was this same need that helped Jews, through hundreds of years, to discover the laws of living together, to do justly, to love mercy and to walk humbly with their God.

THINKING ABOUT WHAT YOU HAVE LEARNED

1. Can you remember a time when you had trouble making a decision on what was the right and what was the wrong thing to do?
2. Would you be satisfied with the answers God gave to Job?

QUESTIONS TO ASK YOUR PARENTS

1. How do your parents feel about the story of Job?
2. Can a man who suffers a calamity today be comforted by Job's story?

CHAPTER XXX

Looking backward to the future

We have been looking backward into the life of our people and we have seen how ways of life change. Your own life is different from that of your parents, just as their life is different from that of their parents. And so on, all the way back in time. In other words, we have been learning from past experience. Why?

The newest, most modern thing

Look at it this way. Suppose you are going to fire a huge rocket. The rocket you want to fire is being built in California and the place you want to fire it from is Cape Canaveral, Florida. First you have to get the rocket from California to Florida. To do this you have to have a special truck or trucks. You have to chart a special route so that you won't get in the way of other travellers on the road. You may have to detour to avoid tunnels that are too small or bridges that won't bear up under the heavy truck and rocket.

Finally you get the rocket to Cape Canaveral and onto the launching pad.

But your preparations aren't over yet for the rocket has to be checked and made ready. This takes not just one or two hours, but many hours. Sometimes it takes a day or more than a day.

At last the rocket is ready. From your watching-place half a mile away you see sparks, then a great burst of flame, then a giant cloud of smoke. The rocket zooms off into space. It makes the loudest noise man has ever known.

As the sleek silver rocket disappears from your view, you may be thinking that this is the newest and most modern thing you can imagine. There seems to be little about the rocket that goes back into past history. But that is not true at all.

We learn from the past

The idea of rockets first began when man looked at a squid and saw that it moved by sucking in water and squirting it out behind him. This was the beginning of a new theory of locomotion. And more than seven hundred and fifty years ago, the Chinese people invented a fire-

185

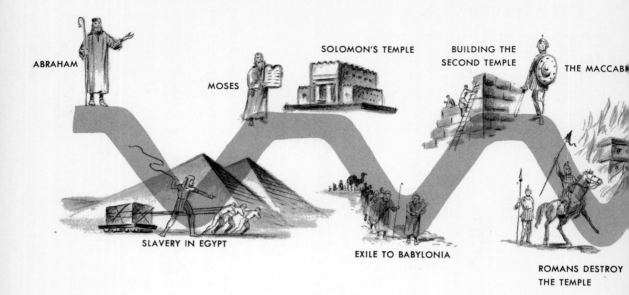

Good times and bad in Jewish history

ABRAHAM

MOSES

SOLOMON'S TEMPLE

BUILDING THE SECOND TEMPLE

THE MACCABI

SLAVERY IN EGYPT

EXILE TO BABYLONIA

ROMANS DESTROY THE TEMPLE

works rocket that moved by a jet of flame that shot out of its tail. You can see that this first flying rocket was the ancestor of all the modern rockets we know today.

But that is not all either. Your big space rocket is flying toward the moon where you aimed it. It will not get to the moon for two days. And to know where the moon would be two days after the rocket left earth, your knowledge has to go back to Galileo, and even before Galileo to astronomers who lived more than two thousand years ago.

Firing a rocket seems hard to do, but it is actually fairly easy. For we know what we want to do and we just have to figure out how to do it. Our past knowledge helps us to figure out the best way.

To live life well, to be a good and just and loving person, is much more complex than firing a rocket. Why is this so? Because people—you and I— are much more complicated and much more complex than the most complicated rocket.

And the guides in our complex life have always been our religion and our past history. We have learned, and must continue to learn through our religion and our past history, how to adapt our lives to the changing times.

As we know, religion provides the goals. We have learned that man wants raisins and almonds and shoes; he wants peace and plenty. Our past, our traditions, our religion pictures these goals for us and gives us tests on how to achieve them and how to reach them.

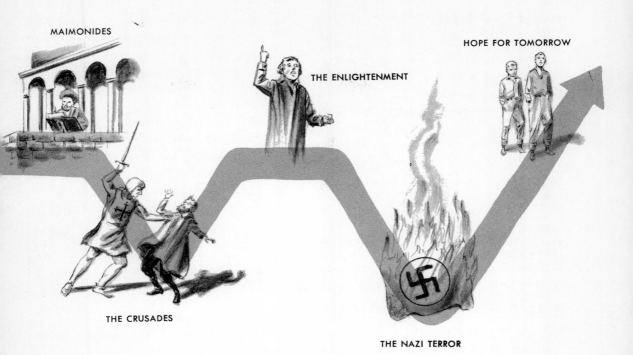

MAIMONIDES

THE ENLIGHTENMENT

HOPE FOR TOMORROW

THE CRUSADES

THE NAZI TERROR

Why man can look ahead

Man is a special creature, made in the image of God, and therefore endowed with the wonderful power to look ahead. Man is not like an animal who is content to stay in any place he knows. Man can think and feel and hope and dream. He can imagine great things. He does not want to stand still.

And because man can think, he has a faith. With the help of his faith, he is able to imagine a time of plenty, a time of goodness and peace. And because he can see this, he feels a need for it and he must have it.

Man discovers new medicines to keep us healthier. Man invents new machines to make our work easier and our lives happier. Man produces rockets and satellites to deepen our knowledge of our world and our universe. All these comforts and all this knowledge are part of our way of seeking our eternal goals. But this is not the whole answer. For a rocket can be used for good or bad, and it is up to man to learn to use the rocket well.

Religion can help us, though it may not have all the answers. But when we look at the lives of our ancestors and find out how they tried to cope with the complex idea of living, we can learn from them. They taught us about God. They gave us the Ten Commandments. They showed us that man was but little lower than the angels, and that his life was precious.

They gave us the one simple answer —"to do justly, to love mercy, and to walk humbly with thy God."

187

Now it is up to you

Our ancestors kept up with the changes that came in the lands where they lived. And now your time is coming to make decisions in the world. As you become a member of the synagogue and of the Jewish community and of the world in which you live, it will be up to you to decide what is right and what is wrong, how to live and how to help your neighbor to live.

Your Judaism will help you to decide. The wisdom of our past will help you to test each new action as you face it. The experience of our past will help you to choose whether something is good or bad for us today.

And the spirit of our past will help you to become better persons and better Jews. For this undying spirit will lead you to strive for the best of worlds: *l'takken olam b'malchut shaddai*—to perfect the world into the Kingdom of God.

THINKING ABOUT WHAT YOU HAVE LEARNED

1. How does a modern rocket depend on the achievements of the past?
2. How can Judaism help us to use scientific achievements for man's good?

QUESTIONS TO ASK YOUR PARENTS

1. Why is man's ability to learn from the past important for the world's future?
2. How will Judaism help me to become a better person?

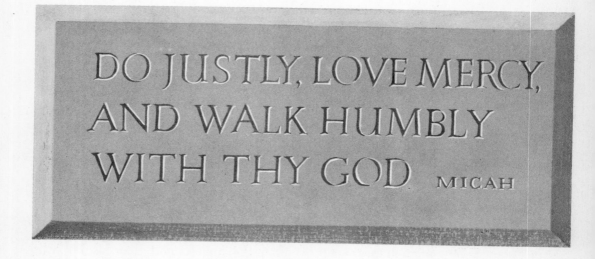

Index